From Stonehenge
to Las Vegas

From Stonehenge to Las Vegas

Archaeology as Popular Culture

Cornelius Holtorf

ALTAMIRA
PRESS

A Division of
ROWMAN & LITTLEFIELD PUBLISHERS, INC.
Walnut Creek • Lanham • New York • Toronto • Oxford

ALTAMIRA PRESS
A division of Rowman & Littlefield Publishers, Inc.
1630 North Main Street, #367
Walnut Creek, CA 94596
www.altamirapress.com

Rowman & Littlefield Publishers, Inc.
A wholly owned subsidiary of The Rowman & Littlefield Publishing Group, Inc.
4501 Forbes Boulevard, Suite 200
Lanham, MD 20706

PO Box 317
Oxford
OX2 9RU, UK

British Library Cataloguing in Publication Information Available

Library of Congress Cataloging-in-Publication Data

Holtorf, Cornelius, 1968–
    From Stonehenge to Las Vegas : archaeology as popular culture / Cornelius Holtorf.
        p.   cm.
    Includes bibliographical references and index.
    ISBN 0-7591-0266-X (Cloth : alk. paper) — ISBN 0-7591-0267-8
(Paper : alk. paper)
    1. Archaeology.   I. Title.
    CC165.H65   2005
    930.1—dc22   2004017780

Printed in the United States of America

∞ ™ The paper used in this publication meets the minimum requirements of American
National Standard for Information Sciences—Permanence of Paper for Printed Library
Materials, ANSI/NISO Z39.48–1992.

CONTENTS

Preface   vii

1 Archaeology and Popular Culture   1
2 Below the Surface   16
3 The Archaeologist in the Field   39
4 Interpreting Traces   60
5 Past Meanings   78
6 Contemporaneous Meanings   92
7 Authenticity   112
8 The Past as a Renewable Resource   130
9 Archaeo-appeal   150

Bibliography   161
Index   177
About the Author   187

PREFACE

This book is an ambitious venture. It reevaluates some fundamentals of the existing discipline of archaeology and its practices, effectively seeking to redefine the academic meaning of the term *archaeology*. My main ambition has been to present the field of archaeology in a new, interesting, and, I hope, timely way. This book is my take on a subject and discipline I have been attracted to and engaged in for more than half of my life.

It may be useful to say a few words about my own intellectual and personal history in order to shed light on how my ideas were shaped and what background I am drawing on. I was born and educated in Germany, where I studied archaeology (*Vor- und Frühgeschichte*), cultural/social anthropology, and physical anthropology in Tübingen and Hamburg, spending one year as a visiting student at the British University of Reading in between. Most of the archaeological lectures I attended at university have been in prehistory, which explains the many prehistoric case studies in this book and my emphasis on the method of excavation rather than the study of standing buildings or landscapes. My master's thesis at Hamburg was concerned with the contemporary meanings of megaliths, employing an ethnographic approach in three case studies (I have drawn from its results in chapter 6). At that time, I began to regret that I had not attended more classes in the discipline of *Empirische Kulturwissenschaft* or *Volkskunde* (with close affinities to European ethnology), especially at Tübingen, where the subject has long been practiced in a particularly exciting way (Bausinger et al. 1978; Maase and Warneken 2003). Some of the literature and basic approaches within that field have since then influenced considerably my own research questions and approaches as represented in this book (see also Gazin-Schwartz and Holtorf 1999). My German academic roots mean that I will occasionally have to refer to German literature in this book since that is what I am drawing on in parts (English translations are not usually available).

Having had a pleasant taste of British archaeology at Reading, I moved to the Welsh town of Lampeter in 1993, where I first gained a master's in archaeological theory and then continued as a research student of Michael Shanks. My doctoral thesis was entitled "Monumental Past: Interpreting the Meanings of Ancient Monuments in Later Prehistoric Mecklenburg-Vorpommern, Germany" (see Holtorf 2000–2004 and parts of chapter 5). The content of that work was partly meant as a sort of allegory for the role of ancient monuments in the present, and for the same reasons as outlined in chapter 1, I had left the borders between past people and present meanings deliberately fuzzy. Since then I have lived, researched, and taught at Göteborg in Sweden, at Cambridge in the United Kingdom, at Stockholm, and now at Lund, having returned to Sweden. Over the last few years, I have gotten involved in new research projects, including among others a large excavation project at Monte Polizzo on the southern Italian island of Sicily, my own excavations at Monte da Igreja in southern Portugal, and an international network project about the archaeology of zoos, which, in one way or another, have all influenced parts of this book.

I would not have been able to complete this book were it not for the support I received from the Department of Archaeology, University of Cambridge, where I was given the privileged position of senior research associate during the 2001–2002 academic year. The book was completed after my move to *Riksantikvarieämbetet*, the Swedish National Heritage Board in Stockholm where I held a Marie Curie Fellowship of the European Commission between 2002 and 2004. I am very grateful to these institutions and the people that make them what they are for their support, and I hope that the latter will enjoy reading the finished book as much as I enjoyed writing it. I must add, however, that the views and arguments in this book are not those of any of these institutions but are mine alone, and I assume full responsibility for any consequences.

A large number of people have encouraged me on my archaeological journey, which has led me in the search for intellectual treasure to investigations in six universities and to discoveries of some pretty exotic ideas in many mysterious places. This book is the result. I would like to thank all my friends and colleagues who have over the years influenced my thinking and supported my research in so many different ways. One person stands out: my former academic teacher Michael Shanks, whose intellectual ingenuity has inspired me for over a decade now. If I could trust my memory better or had kept a diary, I would list many other names here, too. I would especially like to acknowledge the many friends and colleagues who sent their thoughts and suggestions to numerous specific queries I had while writing this book.

Some of the chapters are based on previously published work, but all have been thoroughly edited and revised, if not completely rewritten. Chapter 4 draws on an essay that I contributed (in German) to *Spuren und Botschaften* (Veit et al. 2003). Chapter 5 relies in part on a paper published in *World Archaeology* 1998. Chapter 7 is based on a joint paper with Tim Schadla-Hall in *European Journal of Archaeology* 1999, and I would like to thank Tim for allowing me here to reproduce my own parts of this paper as well as his anecdote about the slingstones for sale at Maiden Castle. Parts of chapter 8 were first published in *Arkeologen* 1998, as well as in revised form in *Destruction and Conservation of Cultural Property* (Layton et al. 2001), whereas chapter 9 contains sections from a paper in *Public Archaeology* 2000.

The bibliography makes no attempt to be complete but contains only such works that I consider particularly significant. I am grateful for permission to cite from (then or still) unpublished material by Britt Arnesen, Charles Bergman, Marvin Cohodas, Knut Ebeling, Matthew Edgeworth, Stephanie Moser, Alexandra Service, Lauren Talalay, Julian Thomas, and Tom Yarrow. For permission to reproduce the images and for help with acquiring good originals, I would like to thank Wilfried Beege, Andrew Cross, Kristina Hagbard, Cole Henley, Judith Kaufmann, Alison Lochhead, Paulien Mulder, Patrick Nagatani, Anne and Patrick Poirier, Nigel Poor, Martin Posselt, Heidi Schierke, and Friederike von Redwitz.

Audiences at the University of the West of England in Bristol, Trinity College in Carmarthen, the University of Stockholm, and the Humboldt University at Berlin have helped me clarify my argument in various places and suggested additional angles to think about. All or parts of earlier versions of the manuscript have been read and commented upon by Håkan Karlsson, Gavin Lucas, Neil Mortimer, Aleks Pluskowski, Martin Schmidt, and Bob Trubshaw. I have benefited enormously from all their comments and suggestions, but especially from the very detailed comments of Aleks Pluskowski and Martin Schmidt. In addition, I had the benefit of reacting to very helpful comments by four anonymous referees, who raised many valuable issues after reading the penultimate version of the entire book. Finally, thanks to Mitch Allen and Susan Scharf at Altamira Press for believing in my project, Andrew Brozyna for a fantastic cover design, and Jen Kelland for attentive copyediting. I am very grateful to Ymke Mulder for preparing the index.

Over the years, Ymke and I have been on our own journey from Stonehenge to Las Vegas. In 1992 we passed in a minibus the amazing prehistoric monument before we even knew we would become a couple. Almost a decade later we got married while staying at the Luxor Hotel in the Nevadan desert. While I was researching and writing this book, Ymke took care of little Tom. What he has been teaching both of us during these first few months, and now years, of his life is that, in final analysis, the most important thing in life is sleep. I therefore dedicate this book to Tom's dreams.

May we all have long and colorful dreams in the future.

CHAPTER ONE

ARCHAEOLOGY AND POPULAR CULTURE

Archaeology is as much a set of experiences . . . as it is a body of meth-
odological principles or techniques.

—Michael Shanks (1995: 25)

Archaeology is a field that fascinates many in the contemporary
Western world. People love to study it, read about it, watch programs about it on TV, observe it, either in action or in exhibitions, and engage with its results. Moreover, we are all surrounded in our
lives by colorful archaeological sceneries appearing in tourist brochures
and on billboards, in cartoons and movies, in folk tales and literary fiction,
in theme parks and at reconstructed ancient sites. Seen in this context,
archaeology is less a way of accessing foreign and distant worlds, removed
from us in time and often also in space, as it is a valued part of our very
own world. Arguably, the "archaeological" has become so significant to
our culture that archaeology can even be considered as a *Leitwissenschaft*
of our time, an academic discipline that guides our age (Schneider 1985:
8; see also Borbein 1981; Ebeling 2004).

Although it may be a fairly small set of distinctive images of archaeology that nonarchaeologists enjoy and make their own, one of the reasons
for the ubiquity of archaeology is that archaeologists not only dig in the
ground but also in a number of significant popular themes (see also
Shanks 2001; Wallace 2004). Often, archaeology acquires a metaphorical
significance. It is some of these themes and metaphors that I shall explore
in this book, for a study of archaeology as it is manifested in popular culture can also tell us a lot about ourselves: it reveals metaphors we think
with, dreams and aspirations we harbor inside ourselves, and attitudes that
inform how we engage not only with ancient sites and objects but with
our surroundings generally. One of the aims of this book, then, is to make

1

a contribution to the cultural anthropology of ourselves. I am asking how it is that archaeology and archaeological objects offer meaningful experiences and rich metaphors to the present Western world.

Collective Memories, History, and the Study of the Past

Archaeology draws some of its appeal and significance from its references to the distant past. The distant past is that beyond living memory, i.e., from the emergence of human beings until circa sixty to eighty years

Figure 1.1   This book was written with a particular attitude towards archaeology. Naturally, not everybody will agree with me. Collage by Cornelius Holtorf.

ago—a period during which many processes and events took place that we find today significant or interesting. Although nobody we could meet today was around at the time, our knowledge of the distant past can be said to be the result of a process of collective remembering (see Holtorf 2000–2004: 2.3).

Through memory we re-present the past, and this applies equally to our respective personal past and to that of our culture, region, or species. Recent sociological studies have tended to take the view that all forms of remembering, whether individual or collective, share a similar dependence on the specific social conditions of those remembering and are thus constructions of their respective presents (see, e.g., Thelen 1989; Fentress and Wickham 1992). Both kinds of memory rely on what we are reminded of or told, as well as on whom or what we trust, in certain situations, and both can acquire acute political and ethical dimensions. The distinction between personal and collective memory thus loses its sharpness and ultimately its relevance. More important are the precise conditions under which memories are constructed and the personal and social implications of the remembered pasts. As the historian David Thelen (1989: 1125) puts it in an influential paper titled "Memory and American History," "In a study of memory the important question is not how accurately a recollection fitted some piece of a past reality, but why historical actors constructed their memories in a particular way at a particular time."

This insight has become the basis for interesting work with and about people recalling events and processes of their own lifetime through the practice of oral history and studies in social remembering (Middleton and Edwards 1990). Similar attention is now being given to the social construction of collective memories of the more distant past. How, for example, dinosaurs (Mitchell 1998), human origins (Moser 1998), megaliths (Holtorf 2000–2004), the Celts (Pomian 1996), ancient Egypt (Frayling 1992; Malamud 2001), ancient Greece and Rome (Himmelmann 1976; James 2001; Dyson 2001), the Etruscans (Thoden van Velzen 1999), the Vikings (Service 1998a, 1998b), or the Middle Ages (Eco 1986: 61–72; Gustafsson 2002) are collectively remembered is increasingly attracting interest among scholars from numerous disciplines (see also the comprehensive collection of papers in Jensen and Wieczorek 2002). Such studies are not only illuminating as contributions to a better understanding of our own (popular) culture. The insights gained from them also have direct

Contemporary Realms of Memory

Between 1984 and 1992 the French publisher Pierre Nora edited a monumental work of seven volumes about the collective memory of France entitled *Les Lieux de Mémoire* (realms of memory): "A *lieu de mémoire* is any
significant entity, whether material or non-material in nature, which by
dint of human will or the work of time has become a symbolic element of
the memorial heritage of any community (in this case, the French community)" (Nora 1996: xvii). Crucially, these realms of memory do not only
include places (e.g., museums, cathedrals, cemeteries, and memorials) but
also concepts and practices (e.g., generations, mottos, and commemorative
ceremonies), as well as objects (e.g., inherited property, monuments, classic
texts, and symbols). In effect, his books have become *lieux de mémoire*, too
(Nora 1996: xix).

According to Nora (1989: 19), all realms of memory are artificial and
deliberately fabricated. Their purpose is "to stop time, to block the work of
forgetting," and they all share "a will to remember." They are not common
in all cultures but a phenomenon of our time: realms of memory replace a
"real" and "true" living memory, which was with us for millennia but has
now ceased to exist. Nora thus argues that a constructed history is now
replacing true memory. He distinguishes true memory, borne by living
societies maintaining their traditions, from artificial history, which is
always problematic and incomplete and represents something that is no
longer present. For Nora, this kind of history holds nothing desirable.

It is clear that archaeological sites, too, are places where memory crystal-
lizes in the present, transporting the past into people's everyday lives (see
chapter 6). Although a specific study of archaeological realms of memory
remains to be written, various contributions to Nora's venture are discussing Palaeolithic cave paintings, megaliths, rock carvings, and the Gauls
(Pomian 1996) as important archaeological *lieux de mémoire*.

Moreover, Lawrence Kritzman suggests in the foreword to the English
edition (Nora and Kritzman 1996: xii) that Nora's quest in itself can be
described as archaeological in as much as he and his contributors seek to
uncover sites of French national memory.

political and ethical bearings on how to engage with communities that remember their own past in terms different from those of the academics, both within and beyond the contexts of the Western world (see, e.g., Layton 1994). Even official policies regarding the preservation of ancient sites are relativized and increasingly being questioned (e.g., Byrne 1991; Wienberg 1999). It appears that the perspectives of academic archaeologists and heritage managers are simply manifestations of particular ways of remembering the past. There are alternatives.

The German historian Jörn Rüsen has over the past decade advanced an interesting argument with regard to history's cultural significance. For him, history is "interpreted time" and encompasses all forms in which the human past is present in a given society (Rüsen 1994a: 6–7). This has two important implications that are both equally applicable to archaeology. First, history is not dependent solely on what really

> **Thesis 1:**
> The important question about memory is why people remember the past in a particular way at a particular time.

happened in the past but also on how it is remembered and actually present in people's minds. The sense of the past is thus quite as much a matter of history as what happened in it—in fact the two are indivisible (Samuel 1994: 15). Later in this book, I will discuss how differently archaeological monuments, and by implication the past, are being understood in our own culture (chapters 5 and 6) and what may follow from an analysis of this variety for the management of ancient sites (chapter 8). Second, history is present in a whole range of human activities and experiences in daily life and not restricted to the content of books or lectures and the presence of ancient sites and monuments.

Rüsen refers to this notion of history as *Geschichtskultur*, which might be translated as "history culture" or "culture of history" (1994b, 1994c). Rüsen's notion of *Geschichtskultur* replaces the notion of an objective historical scholarship that could be independent from its cultural conditions and contexts. Instead, all manifestations of history in a given society, including those in academic forms, are equally considered to be elements of a certain "culture of history." They function within different "theatres of memory" (Samuel 1994), and they deserve equal attention by historians. As a consequence, Rüsen's students have investigated phenomena as diverse as historic memorials, history in advertising, and the significance of political commemoration days. This approach to history is similar to my own in relation to archaeology.

There is one important question that arises not only from Rüsen's argument but also from the recent studies about remembering I mentioned. If so much emphasis lies on the past in the present, what are the implications for future academic research about the past?

As far as I am concerned, the practices of archaeology in the present are far more important and also more interesting than what currently accepted scientific methods can teach us about a time long past. Much of what actually happened hundreds or thousands of years ago is either scientifically inaccessible in its most significant dimensions, inconclusive in its relevance, or simply irrelevant to the world in which we are living now. Archaeology, however, remains significant, not because it manages to import actual past realities into the present but because it allows us to recruit past people and what they left behind for a range of contemporary human interests, needs, and desires. That significance of archaeology is what this book is about.

Professional archaeology consists of various present-day practices, including advancing academic discourse, teaching students, managing tourist sites, archives, or museum collections, and administering or investigating archaeological sites in the landscape. These practices are governed entirely by the rules, conventions, and ambitions of our present society and relate to its established values, norms, procedures, and genres. For example, research is valued in the form of completed publications and persuasive arguments, investigations in the form of comprehensive and informative reports, teaching in the form of cognitive- and social-learning outcomes, and management in the form of apparent care, efficiency, and accountability. Although all of these activities depict the past in some form, a time traveler's observations about the degree to which these depictions relate to what it was actually like in the past remains largely irrelevant. Importantly, I am not denying the relevance of the past to the present categorically; I merely question the significance of accurately knowing the past in the present (see also chapter 8).

The only significant exceptions where the past matters more immediately today are archaeological studies whose results can be literally applied to present needs. A classic example is Clark Erickson's applied archaeology research investigating the ancient "raised fields" in the Lake Titicaca region of Peru and Bolivia, which can help contemporary farmers develop techniques for growing crops on fields that now lie fallow (as discussed with Kris Hirst 1998). These agricultural projects will stand or fall, in part, with the quality of the archaeological science on which they are based. Other examples could be drawn from long-term predictions of environmental or evolutionary changes, which likewise rely in part on accurate knowledge available about past conditions and developments. In the overwhelming majority of cases, however, it is not what happened in the past that needs investigating but why so many of us are so interested in the past in the first place and what role archaeology plays in relation to that interest.

Why should anybody want to know how people actually lived their lives during past millennia? How can a profession excavating old "rubbish" gain scientific credibility, social respect, and a fair amount of popular admiration? Why do fairly arcane archaeological details and hypotheses interest anyone other than specialists? Why are so many ancient artifacts kept in museums and sites preserved in the landscape? How can it possibly be so important to try to "rescue" ancient sites from how we collectively choose to develop our land? In short, why do people love archaeology and the past it is investigating? To answer questions such as these, what matters are the meanings of the past in the present, how archaeological sites and artifacts relate to them, and the specific roles archaeology is playing in contemporary society and its popular culture. This book begins to explore some of these issues.

Archaeology in Popular Culture

I need to say a few words here about what I mean by popular culture and how I will be studying it since this is a controversial field (for overviews see Maltby 1989; Storey 2001). For me, the most important aspect of popular culture is neither its popularity (some refer to "mass culture") nor its homogeneity as a culture ("folk culture" as opposed to "high culture"). I like the way some German folklorists employ the term *Alltagskultur* ("everyday culture"), referring to whatever characterizes the way people live their daily lives and problematizing what is usually taken for granted (Bausinger et al. 1978). I also like a similar definition of popular culture offered by Raymond Williams (1976: 199), one of the fathers of cultural studies in Britain. He describes it as "the culture actually made by people for themselves," thus excluding, for example, what they do for their employers. In this sense, popular culture refers to how people choose to live their own lives, how they perceive and shape their local environments through their actions, and what they find appealing or interesting. For example, Indiana Jones may not first come to mind when professional archaeologists consider what they do, but it is certainly high on the list of other people's associations with archaeology (see chapter 3). Likewise, for professionals or others who spotted it, the "Khuza" culture may have been a cunning hoax around a collection of faked archaeological evidence, but for the unsuspecting public the exhibition represented nothing but yet another ancient culture with associated authentic artifacts (see chapter 7). Ultimately, however, the perceptions of the many matter as much, or more, than the factual knowledge of the few, especially since that factual knowledge, too, is not really privileged but simply based on one particular perception of archaeology, archaeological objects, and perhaps the world (see chapters 5 and 6).

Richard Maltby (1989: 14), a professor of screen studies at Flinders University, states that "popular culture is a form of dialogue society has with itself." It expresses—and reproduces—our inner thoughts and emotions, our (supposedly) secret fears and desires, and our favorite habits and behaviors. Popular culture is helping us to recognize ourselves in the lives we lead. In this sense it is about actively producing culture as much as about passively consuming commodities (cf. Fiske 1989; Schulze 1993). Partly this culture is the same among very many people, but it can also be very diverse. In some respects, the culture people produce is diverse and dependent on whether they are rich or poor, well or poorly educated, but in other respects all may share the same culture. Sometimes it appears that people's actions and preferences are highly predictable and manipulated, but at other times they are surprising and challenging. In this book I am not interested in developing such analytic distinctions (see, e.g., Schulze 1993) but in exploring one aspect of the richness of Western popular culture in its own right.

Adapting Williams's phrase, one could say that I am looking at how people are actually making archaeology for themselves. This does not mean, of course, that anybody could actually make his or her own archaeology in complete isolation from what is already available, for example due to the productivity of archaeologists, writers, and producers. It rather means that in creating culture, all of us are constantly making significant choices, by preferring some ideas, sites, artifacts, texts, or images to others. These choices are not arbitrary but the results of values and attitudes that are largely acquired during socialization and reaffirmed by the choices of others (see Fluck 1987). Archaeologists, too, are people and make such choices, but since their own views of archaeology are abundantly documented in the academic and educational literature, I am focusing here mostly on nonarchaeologists. They are the people who surround me in my daily life, who read some of the same novels, watch some of the same TV programs, and visit some of the same tourist sites as I do, as well as some others. Most of them I will probably never get to know, but some I meet. In addition, I include the work and perspectives of a few individuals who, although not archaeologists themselves, have impressed me through their work on archaeology: they are academics from other fields, filmmakers, authors, or visual artists. I have been observing all these people and consuming their work with an anthropological approach, trying to understand meanings by attentively watching, listening, and reading.

My temporal frame of reference in this book is related to my own age and covers more or less the last two decades, with some excursions into the more distant past. My geographical scope is the Western world (see figure 1.2). It is very clear that the situation in other parts of the world would require an altogether different argument and other aspirations (see Byrne 1991; Shepherd 2002; Stille 2002). My own life has featured substantial episodes in Germany, England, Wales, and Sweden; I have traveled widely in Europe and been a few times to North America and other continents. Personal experiences in all these places have informed this work. Quite possibly, some of my argument will make sense in an area larger than where it originally derives from. Such is the impact of globalization that not only certain general themes but also some specific cultural items have spread widely.

There can be no doubt that some very powerful forces of cultural assimilation are at work across the globe. Their impact appears to be especially large where the commercial potential is large too, e.g., in TV programming and in the urban entertainment industries. But other, far less commercial phenomena, such as the spread of esoteric thinking, underline this trend too. It is therefore becoming more and more difficult to know

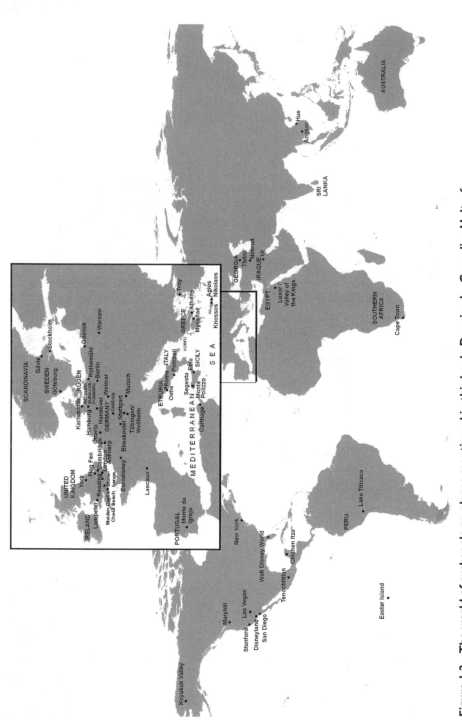

Figure 1.2 The world of archaeology: places mentioned in this book. Drawing by Cornelius Holtorf.

precisely what may be American or Swedish or Welsh or German popular culture, and at the same time it becomes less and less useful to try and split apart what is growing together. Regarding the various examples given in this book, I see therefore no great benefit from getting into the subtleties of precisely who owns or can relate to which element of popular culture. This is not to deny the continuing significance of certain cultural distinctions, for example those related to specific regional traditions and specific languages, or the widespread interest in maintaining such particularities, sometimes precisely by employing archaeological sites or objects. Here, though, I do not wish to explore the popular concepts of archaeology in specific Western cultures but the specific concepts of archaeology in Western popular culture.

How people have known ancient objects in their own terms is not a new topic but has been studied previously by scholars interested in the folklore of archaeological artifacts and monuments. Now contemporary understandings of the same sites are given equal attention. The anthropologist Jerome Voss (1987) and the folklorist Wolfgang Seidenspinner (1993), for example, both argued that popular archaeological interpretations featuring alignments of ancient sites in the landscape (so-called ley-lines), visitors from outer space, prehistoric calendars, computers, and astronomical observatories can be seen as the folklore of our age. Such interpretations are a part of what has been called "folk archaeology" (Michlovic 1990), and usually they rely on approaches and methods very different from those of academic archaeology (see Cole 1980). A number of archaeologists and anthropologists consider popular folk archaeology as a threat to the values and prospects of scientific archaeology in society. Kenneth Feder (1999), for example, spent considerable time and effort discussing the flaws of what he calls "pseudoscience." He argued in detail that theories such as those about the exploration and settlement of the Americas after the indigenous populations and before Columbus, the sunken Atlantis, visits to Earth by ancient astronauts, dowsing as an archaeological method, and the literal truth of the biblical creation story are deeply flawed and ultimately even dangerous since they mislead people about the past and discredit modern science.

Archaeologists sometimes assume that people's occasional indifference and apathy towards the true ambitions of academic archaeology are due to a void in peoples' minds where knowledge and understanding should reside. In reality, what archaeology intends is often not education but reeducation for its own (dubious) purposes (Byrne 1995: 278). Michael Michlovic (1990) pointed out that patronizing reactions towards folk archaeology are merely the result of a perceived challenge to archaeology's monopoly on interpretation of the past and the associated state support. It would be more appropriate, he argued, to understand the cultural context from which such alternative theories emerge and the genuine needs to which they respond. In other words, archaeologists should appreciate alternative approaches for what they are rather than for what they are not.

In a recent book about archaeology and science fiction, Miles Russell (2002: 38) observed it is astonishing that given archaeologists' obsession with context in the past, they do not tend to be very knowledgeable about their very own context today: how their methodology and subject matter is perceived and what their role within society is widely thought to be. Yet, arguably academic archaeology owes its own existence and establishment to a widely shared popular fascination with archaeology, rather than vice versa. Folk archaeology can lead professional archaeologists to the actual social realities within which any kind of archaeology is practiced today. This book makes a contribution to understanding better these realities by investigating some of the themes and motifs that make archaeology thrive in the contemporary Western world.

The widespread popularity of archaeology and archaeological sites or artifacts has meant that they have entered many different realms and discourses, only some of which can be called academic. They range from folklore (Liebers 1986) to tomb robbing (Thoden van Velzen 1996, 1999) and from contemporary art (Putnam 2001) to alternative "sciences" and religions (Chippindale et al. 1990). (Pre-)historical novels are a further example. It has been suggested that they do not simply fill in the gaps left in academic archaeological reconstructions but constitute their own meaningful universe (Wetzel 1988). Novels can thus usurp the very procedures and status of archaeology itself, effectively assuming its place in certain contexts. In this view academic archaeology is one of many systems of meaning, none of which has a monopoly on "reality."

Archaeology as Popular Culture

A second main aim of this book is to suggest a new understanding of professional archaeology itself, shifting the emphasis from archaeology as a way of learning about the past to archaeology as a set of relations (to the surface, gender roles, material clues, artifacts, monuments, originals, the past, among many others) in the present.

Currently, academics and many others tend to assume that archaeology is essentially about bridging the gulf between the past and present (see figure 1.3). Archaeologists use a wide range of (more or less) sophisticated techniques and methodologies in their research designs in order to make ancient finds and features "speak" and "give up" their "secrets" so that we can all learn more about the past. In this view, every generation of archaeologists builds on the existing body of knowledge and adds to it so that our knowledge of the past improves continuously. Archaeology thus appears as a specialized craft mastered by experts who enjoy considerable

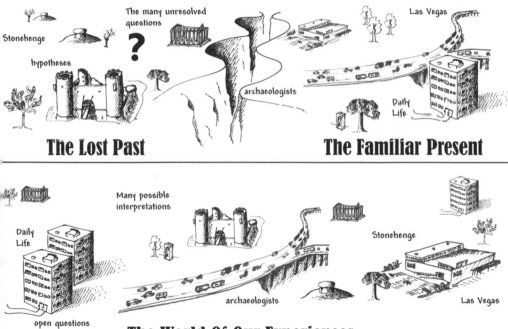

Figure 1.3 Two views of archaeology: (top) the gulf between past and present realities, with archaeologists seeking a bridge; (bottom) past and present as part of a single reality, with archaeologists and others celebrating it. Drawing by Cornelius Holtorf.

authority concerning past human cultures. Their supposed expertise lies in knowing the past and its remains, being able to explain long-term changes, and comprehending at least some of past people's "otherness." Traditionally, the archaeologists' self-adopted brief is therefore that of the scholar who can supply answers to questions about the past but sometimes also that of the cultural critic, challenging familiar notions and apparent certainties in the present with insights gained about the past.

I wish to challenge the dominant view by undermining its very foundation. In discussing the popular elements of modern archaeology and a number of powerful archaeological themes, I suggest an alternative categorization of archaeology: from archaeology as science and scholarship to archaeology as popular culture. This change of allegiance, like others suggested previously (see table 1.1), is much more than a semantic exercise. As will become clear throughout this book, I am proposing a novel, general theory of archaeology rather than simply more theory for archaeology. I am arguing that archaeology can and should be seen in the context and, indeed, in the terms in which it is appreciated in contemporary popular culture. The widespread fascination with both the past and the practice of archaeology (what I call "archaeo-appeal" in chapter 9) is the ultimate reason and justification for why it exists in the way it does. The gulf my discussion bridges, if any, is thus not that between the present and a lost past but between professional and academic realms, on the one hand, and other, especially popular, ways of appreciating and engaging with the past in the present, on the other hand.

My argument is based on the supposition that archaeology, in all its

Table 1.1 Allegiances of archaeology.

Archaeology as . . .	Key references
science / scholarship	Feder 1999; common archaeological textbooks
academic discourse	Shanks 1990, 1996; Tilley 1990
theatre / performance	Pearson and Shanks 2001
politics	Tilley 1989a
management	Cooper et al. 1995
craft	Edgeworth 2003; Shanks and McGuire 1996
visual art	Metken 1977; Renfrew 2003
popular culture	This book!

various manifestations, does not offer a perspective from which our own present can be understood in the light of its past. Instead, archaeology offers a perspective from which the past and its remains can be experienced and understood in the light of our present. Similar positions have been advocated or implied by various other archaeologists (e.g., Wilk 1985; Shanks 1992; Tilley 1993; Barrett 1994; Schnapp 1996; Renfrew 2003), and it enjoys a certain currency also among historians and others (e.g., Lowenthal 1985). I found it nevertheless astonishing that according to a recent survey of more than six hundred historians (www.h-debate.com/encuesta/menu.htm, accessed October 1, 2004), as many as 56 percent agreed "quite" or "very much" with the statement, "All history is contemporary," and 53 percent agreed only a little or not at all with the statement, "History is to know the past as it was."

> **Thesis 2:**
> Archaeology is mainly about our own culture in the present.

I suggest in this introductory chapter that archaeology is a much broader cultural field than the narrowly defined specializations the academic world suggest. Archaeology today plays a significant part in Western popular culture at large. It is largely about things that are familiar rather than foreign to us. In the following chapters I explore in some detail how "the archaeological" (Shanks 1995, 2001) manifests itself in our own daily surroundings and discuss what this might imply for the practice of archaeology as a subject and as a profession.

With a nod to Pierre Nora (see sidebar above), I might describe the subject matter of the present book as the realms of archaeology, *les lieux d'archéologie*. I will visit a range of particularly important realms of archaeology, assessing their significance within popular culture and reassessing professional archaeology in light of that significance. These realms include, among others, the sphere of the underground, the perils of fieldwork, the discovery of treasure, the study of traces as clues, the meanings of artifacts and monuments, the notion of authenticity, the belief in the past and past remains as a nonrenewable resource, and the general appeal of "the archaeological." The first realm to be discussed is perhaps the most basic aspect of archaeological practice: its concern with what lies below the surface.

CHAPTER TWO
BELOW THE SURFACE

Below the surface, there are things great and small.
Below the surface, there are laughter and tears.
There is much that happens there which we do not understand,
but we always find the answers,
deep down, within ourselves.

—Uno Svenningsson

That archaeologists investigate what lies below the surface is usually taken for granted. Whereas it has become widely accepted that dug-up ancient objects have a wide range of possible symbolic connotations, the underground itself is still considered little else than a passive container of such meaningful objects. Archaeologists know that various geological, chemical, and other conditions underground can physically preserve, alter, or destroy archaeological objects, but they know far less about the cultural conditions of the underground that likewise affect what can be found.

In Western culture underground worlds have been metaphorically highly charged (see Lesser 1987; Williams 1990; Maase and Warneken 2003; Thomas 2004: chapter 7). According to the linguist George Lakoff and the philosopher Mark Johnson, the up/down division is one of the central metaphors we live by (see table 2.1). Such metaphorical orientations are not at all arbitrary but have a basis in the particular physical and cultural experiences of humans. Archaeological practice contributes to these symbolic connotations as much as they in turn become manifest in some aspects of archaeological excavations (consider figures 2.1 and 3.4). This remains significant, even though not all archaeological sites are underground and not all archaeologists excavate.

It may at first appear trivial to belabor such basic linguistic metaphors in relation to archaeology, but it is significant that archaeology and our culture at large appear to share a similar way of conceptualizing the world in ups and downs. The British archaeologist Michael Shanks (1992: 24) applies the term *tree-thinking* in this context: "In tree-thinking we need

Table 2.1 The basic orientational metaphor of up/down and some of its speculative meanings both in anglophone culture generally and in archaeology specifically (first two columns adapted from Lakoff and Johnson 1980: 14–24).

UP	DOWN	'Down' in archaeology
		Conditions for archaeological work:
foreseeable future events (*What's coming up this week?*)		the past lies below; 'deep time'
unknown (*That's up in the air*)	known, completed (*The matter is settled*)	our past is waiting to be rediscovered.
more (*Turn the heat up!*)	less (*These figures have gone down*)	decaying remains
		What archaeologists find:
conscious (*Wake up*)	unconscious (*He fell asleep*)	revealing lost truths
finished (*The time is up*)		ever more discoveries
virtue (*They have high standards*)	depravity (*That would be beneath me*)	
high status (*She'll rise to the top*)	low status (*He's at the bottom of the social hierarchy*)	indications for the everyday life of ordinary people
	mundane reality (*They are down to earth*)	
health/life (*He's in top shape; she rose from the dead*)	sickness/death (*She came down with flu; he dropped dead*)	dead bodies, burials
good (*Things are looking up; high-quality*)	bad (*Things have gone downhill and are at an all-time low*)	historical progress from poor beginnings to an advanced present
		What archaeologists do:
having control (*She's in a superior position*)	having lost control (*He is under my control; fell in trance*)	applying rigorous research methodologies to what lies below
being rational, reason (*We had a high-level intellectual discussion*)	being emotional (*He couldn't rise above his emotions*)	comtemplating the past, its remains, and dead bodies
happy (*I'm feeling up*)	sad (*I fell into a depression*)	

Figure 2.1   Moving downwards. Claes Oldenburg's *Trowel* (1971). Photograph: Collectie Kröller-Müller Museum, Otterlo, the Netherlands, reproduced by permission.

to dig deep to find origins and our identities." In tree-thinking we are also distinguishing attitudes that are "down-to-earth" and thus controllable and *under*standable from "high-flying" theories and interpretations that deal with what is uncertain and unknown. This may sound self-evident to us but only because the existing alternative conceptualizations are so little used. The philosophers Mark Taylor and Esa Saarinen (1994: interstanding 1–2), for example, argue that in our age *under*standing has become impossible because nothing stands *under* anything else anymore: "When depth gives way to surface, under-standing becomes inter-standing. To comprehend is no longer to grasp what lies beneath but to glimpse what lies between."

This thought is related to so-called rhizomatic thinking that moves not vertically but horizontally, constantly establishing new connections sidewise and being impossible to pin *down* (see Shanks 1992: 35–36; Holtorf 2000–2004: 3.3). Rhizomes are not built on firm roots from which structures grow organically, but they consist of a growing number of constituent parts that establish lateral interconnections. Laterally is also the general direction in which the argument in this book moves. I am not systematically seeking to get to the *bottom* of things, but I will circumscribe my topic by moving from one issue and example to the next.

In the remaining part of this chapter, I discuss several main characteristics of the underground with resonances in a wide range of fields, including archaeology. The subsequent chapter then specifically discusses how discoveries are made through archaeological fieldwork and what risks are involved in getting to these treasures.

The Underground: Literal and Metaphorical

The underground is below the surface and therefore usually invisible to the naked eye. The sheer sensation of depth can nevertheless exert a powerful influence on our senses on the surface. The actress Kate Winslet, for example, expresses this idea in a March 12, 2000, interview with *The Observer*:

> I had a real fear of being in deep water. Of what was below the surface.
> . . . So I learned to scuba-dive—I have to face my fears—and now I feel

19

fine and in control down there. I'm still scared of being on the surface, with all the depth under me. It's like a thin-ice thing I suppose.

Something similar may be sensed when one is standing on top of a cave, beside an enormous abyss, or near an outpouring of hot lava (figure 2.2). Suddenly the surfaces on which we normally move around feeling safe and confident reveal themselves as fragile, shaky, and uncertain. We are completely at the mercy of the powers beneath: "The immensity of time, as well as that of space, arouses fear and awe, the shudder that arises from the apprehension of one's unimportance and impotence before grand natural powers." (Williams 1990: 87)

That depth should be linked to time, as suggested in the preceding quote, is, however, not self-evident. Usually the geologist James Hutton

Figure 2.2   Etna (Sicily, Italy), an entrance to the underground. The key to everything here lies below our feet, beneath layers of ash. As on archaeological sites, this place is characterized by what once happened here and by what could happen here again (and indeed has happened since the picture was taken). The surprise element. Scientists monitor everything. Off-road vehicles. Expert guides lead us further up the mountain and show us around. The smell of sulfur, the heat near the flowing lava. The foundations of this planet erupting to the surface. Everybody takes rocks as souvenirs. Photograph by Cornelius Holtorf, 1999.

(1726–1797) is credited with the discovery of "deep time," or the "abyss of time." He recognized that decay of geological layers on the surface can be reversed and land restored to its original height by forces of elevation. If uplift can thus invert geological erosion and restore the earth's topography to its original height, the age of the earth would appear to have no necessary beginning and the layers of rock simply to represent the most recent history of the earth (see Gould 1987: chapter 3). In a similar way, others began at that time to understand the processes that shaped the landscape as we find it today. Whereas some ancient sites and surfaces had become buried under subsequent cultural deposits or soil, others had been subjected to heavy erosion and eventually disappeared. These processes would later become one of the most fundamental principles for planning and interpreting the results of archaeological fieldwork.

What archaeology thus shares with geology is the basic equation of depth with age, although local circumstances often make the actual calculations far more complex. This principle can be understood better with reference to the second basic idea shared by archaeologists and geologists: the insight that the underground is composed of layers of strata laid down in a regular way. Understanding these layers, the local stratigraphy, is the key to understanding the history of a site. But although the principle is simple enough, establishing stratigraphies of subsequent layers can be difficult due to both erosion and later events that affected earlier deposits. Whereas geologists have to take the impact of fault lines and erosion into account, archaeologists must consider in particular later movements of soil, for example during large-scale leveling, the digging and refilling of pits, and the impact of natural forces such as earthquakes and landslides. It can help to identify certain key fossils or artifacts that are distinctive for particular strata. Such finds were considered early on to form a record of past processes and events from which these, in turn, can be inferred (Patrick 1985: 33–34). The notion that the past lies beneath, i.e., deep time, is significant to the present day.

Since Hutton's time, historians, archaeologists, and others have occasionally felt a shudder when contemplating the mighty pasts beneath their feet. The classicist Theodor Birt, for instance, realized once in the center of the Greek city of Athens "that we stand on the most original classical soil. Precisely here were also the lively ancient market and the bazaars where the maids of Aspasia went for their shopping. Now the floor is raised and the ancient life took place 10 to 20 feet below" (cited in Zint-zen 1998: 38; my translation[1]).

In many cases we have to guess or accept on faith what exactly lies below the surface, but under specific conditions more certainty is attainable. Remote sensing techniques now allow visual access to the underground, although sometimes it is not clear whether plotted geophysical results have actually established the desired clarity or simply created additional mystery (figure 2.3).

Immediate physical access requires digging. Archaeological excavation is only one context within which it can be essential to enter the underground physically. For far longer, people have been mining the earth for various natural resources such as flint, copper, and gold. Mining was where the literal underground merged early on with the metaphorical underground, the symbolic connotations of the act of digging holes into the earth itself have been prominent throughout the history of mining (see Eliade 1962: 45–57; Merchant 1980: chapter 1). Caves too have been attracting strong symbolic interpretations, possibly since people applied cave paintings to them during the Upper Palaeolithic as in the famous cave of Lascaux in France. Still today, most visitors are struck by a sense of awe when they enter unexpectedly large underground spaces and contemplate the skill and endurance of the miners, the accomplishments of the people who dwelled in caves, or the curious shapes of the stalagmites and stalactites.

The strong symbolic significance of the underground has been explored throughout Western literature, from Virgil to Jules Verne and H. G. Wells and from Dante to C. S. Lewis and Mark Twain (see Lesser 1987). Some of the most influential literary pieces of this kind were written at the time of the great archaeological discoveries, and it is therefore unsurprising that they make explicit reference to the discovery of ancient remains and creatures. In Jules Verne's *Journey to the Centre of the Earth* ([1864] 1994), for example, the geology professor Otto Lidenbrock and his nephew, together with a guide, discover while on the way down to the center of the earth not only various prehistoric sea creatures that live in a

---

1. Original German text: "dass wir auf dem echtesten classischen Boden stehen. Gerade hier war auch das antike Marktleben und die Bazare, wo die Mägde Aspasiens ihre Einkäufe machten. Nun ist der Boden aufgehöht und das antike Leben spielte sich 10 bis 20 Fuss tiefer ab."

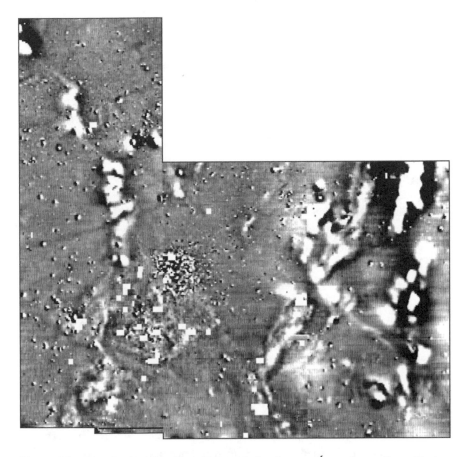

Figure 2.3 Geophysics plot from Monte da Igreja near Évora in southern Portugal. Establishing desired clarity or creating additional mystery about what lies below? Plot by Martin Posselt for Cornelius Holtorf.

large underground lake but also the dead body and possibly a living specimen of a man of the Quaternary Period. Starting with *At the Earth's Core* ([1914] 2000), Edgar Rice Burroughs wrote a series of novels set in Pellucidar, which lies inside the earth's hollow interior. In this vast land, time stands still since their sun never sets, and evolution has taken a different course with some prehistoric animal species and people still alive.

According to MIT historian Rosalind Williams (1990: chapter 2) the descent to the underworld, which is one of the most important Western myths, even inspired scientific quests to recover the truth about the past by digging ever deeper. As I am editing this paragraph I read a newspaper article titled "Life Started Deep Down in the Underground," describing microbes as "Sweden's true first inhabitants": "three billion years ago microbes ruled the planet," but now Swedish scientists are drilling deep into the rock and, in a special laboratory built 450 meters beneath the surface, they are discovering the secrets of their microbe ancestors. In examples like this, we find, Williams writes,

> mythological overtones to the scientific enterprise. Two centuries of scientific excavation after Bacon's death revealed a past of gigantic reptiles, buried cities, fabulous treasures, and apelike humans. As Huxley noted, this is the stuff that dreams are made of. Both in its process and in its results, then, both in the enterprise of digging into subterranean spaces and in what it has found there, modern science acts in an enchanted world. (1990: 49)

These remarks ring particularly true also for the life and work of Heinrich Schliemann (1822–1890) (cf. Lesser 1987: 69–76). His endeavors attracted much attention among wide audiences, who enjoyed following Schliemann's mythic quest at the Turkish site of Troy, attempting to prove right Homer's account of the Trojan War. In the process, Schliemann reinvented even his own biography in mythical terms. For many years and possibly until today, it has been Schliemann's belief in myth and the bright light of his personal journey and apparent success that falls also on other archaeologists' careers and projects, including those that might at first appear to be very prosaic (cf. Zintzen 1998: chapter 7; Wallace 2004: chapter 5).

It is not always the actual finds and features archaeologists discover that capture the imaginations of their audiences. The sheer sense of revealing things below the surface can be equally fascinating. In fact, the appeal of a site occasionally appears to be even greater while the treasures have not (yet) been revealed and only exist in our imaginations. Archaeological documentaries can thrive seemingly forever on contemplations such as, Will the team be able to find the answers to their quest? Will this site reveal its secrets? It seems that the point is never to find an answer but to keep the mystery alive and continue the search. For, as the Galician writer Álvaro Cunqueiro puts it, "As long as there is talk of hidden gold, the possibility of happiness remains alive in us, and we shall be richer for this belief than for possessing all the hidden treasures in the world" (cited in Martinón-Torres 2002: 234).

Such treasures of the imagination cannot be lifted or they lose their power (see Holtorf 2001). With reference to these incredibly rich cultural resonances of the underground, Wendy Lesser (1987: 3), editor of the literary magazine *The Threepenny Review*, states,

> The underground is itself an excellent metaphor for metaphor. It is, on the one hand, a real place in the world, and on the other hand, it is an idea or a feeling: the physical place seems inherently suggestive of the spiritual or literary connotations, and those connotations in turn enrich our experience of the material object. Like all good metaphors, the underground is simultaneously and inseparably a concrete thing and an abstract notion.

The same could be said about archaeology. It is a concrete activity and an abstract notion, often linked to heroic quests. Archaeology has provided some powerful metaphors, and Cambridge science historian Cathy Gere (2002: 195) has argued even that archaeology was a metaphor almost before it had constituted itself as an academic discipline (I discuss specific examples both in this and the following chapters). Most fundamentally, metaphorical archaeology accesses the deep in order to find the past. More specifically, it also searches for treasure.

Hidden Treasures

That the underground contains treasure becomes clear when visiting caves, where guides, information brochures, or stunningly arranged lighting effects invariably suggest that they be interpreted either as spectacular wonders and treasures of nature or as beautiful cathedral architecture and sculpture. For example, a 2001 leaflet of Wookey Hole Caves in Somerset, England, invites visitors on an "awe-inspiring journey into the Earth" exploring "Somerset's buried treasure"; what is more, these caves "have yet to give up all their secrets." Underground treasures are a widespread metaphorical idea, but early antiquarians as well as treasure hunters in all times have tended to take this literally (see, e.g., Martinón-Torres 2002).

As a result, many sites, especially barrows, have been dug up and robbed of their content before archaeologists have had the opportunity to study and excavate them in their preferred methodical way. Finding treasure below the surface is, however, a desire that it is much more deeply rooted than the archaeologists' anger about lost opportunities for their own research.

I recently bought for little money a small book entitled *Treasure Hunting for All: A Popular Guide to a Profitable Hobby* (Fletcher 1973). Given the vast numbers of coins lost over the centuries, Fletcher claims that "professional treasure hunters can confidently claim that there is sufficient money in the ground to pay off the National Debt" (1973: 6). He suggests starting the hunt by digging in your own furniture:

> An average three-piece suite should hold ten coins—four in the settee and three in each chair—if it has not been searched by a previous owner. . . . It also means that if the face value of the coins in an average three-piece suite is as low as ten new pence, no less than £20,000 could be found in a city such as London. (Fletcher 1973: 8)

This is reminiscent of the many folk tales and sagas about treasures hidden in ancient mounds. They once promised the poor social change and a better future through acquisition of material wealth. The British archaeologist Leslie Grinsell listed in a classic paper (1967) a number of examples of prehistoric barrows associated with tales about treasures and, when excavated, indeed yielded objects made from various kinds of precious metals, including Roman coins, a gold cup, a bronze table, and Pictish silverware. But such folk traditions are, of course, not always accurate, and the finds that can be made are not always precious in a monetary sense. Nevertheless, public authorities are still influenced by the notion of archaeological finds and features as treasure. As the Italian etruscologist Massimo Pallottino (1968: 73) pointed out, this is reflected in special laws regulating the "ownership" of sites and artifacts, especially the notion of the "treasure trove" (Grinsell 1967), and in the general understanding of ancient sites and objects as valuable "inheritance" (*heritage, Kulturerbe, kulturarv, patrimonio*, etc.).

Thesis 3:
Archaeology is about searching and finding treasure underground.

Nowadays archaeological treasures do not necessarily refer to great monetary value. It has become customary to state that the daily business of archaeologists is very different from such "treasure hunting" and much more prosaic (e.g., Ross 1980: 9). Modern archaeology is not primarily about recovering monetary valuables and much more about very mundane information, the scientific value of which can be infinitely bigger than that of precious metals. The appeal of scientific facts is different but can be no less attractive to the initiated. TV archaeologists Tony Robinson and Mick Aston (2002: 77) state it succinctly:

> If Tutankhamun's tomb were to be opened for the first time today, archaeologists would be as interested in the information provided by the dust on the floor as they would be in the golden chariots. One golden chariot is pretty much like another, but the dust can tell you about the fortunes of a whole civilization.

In this sense, the thrill of discovering treasure is still something that inspires both students and professionals to do archaeology. Pallottino (1968: 12, 73), for example, justifies continuous archaeological excavating by "the fact that, in the subsoil of lands where antique civilizations flourished, there are still hidden vast treasuries of buried evidence"; after all, "in the last analysis, [the archaeologist] too dreams of 'treasure'" (see figure 2.4). By the same token, the archaeologist Francis Pryor's account of three decades of digging in the fens in Eastern England contains frequent references to significant material "discoveries" he has made and the occasional "jackpot" he has hit. Pryor refers neither to monetary value nor to any aesthetic characteristics but to the potential of particular artifacts and other material evidence for archaeological explanation and storytelling (see Pryor 2001: 22–23, 35, 38). Unfortunately, not all of Pryor's finds have had the same potential, and therefore they have not attracted the same kind of enthusiasm:

> I was feeling already a bit low, but this display of scrappy potsherds, like so many crumbs of wet digestive biscuit, together with mis-shaped pieces of clay "daub" and nondescript splinters of bone was, quite frankly, pathetic. It was almost more than I could bear. . . . "There," I'll announce, "that's what you paid thousands of dollars to discover." No, I couldn't bear it—it was too depressing for words (Pryor 2001: 32).

Figure 2.4   Discovery of a Ford Woody, near the entrance to Lascaux Cave, Dordogne, France 1994/1999, by Patrick Nagatani. From a series of images which are the only surviving records of discoveries made during secret excavations by the enigmatic Japanese archaeologist Ryoichi. Photograph by Patrick Nagatani, reproduced by permission.

Pryor (2001: 3) mentions that as a schoolboy he was inspired by reading about Howard Carter's discovery of Tutankhamun's tomb: "I soon found myself completely gripped by the story of the discovery of the boy king's mummified body and the fabulous treasures which surrounded him. As I read, I was there, amidst the sands of the Nile and the eerie, cool, dry darkness of the tomb."

I do not mention this to criticize Francis Pryor for what reads like very honest descriptions of how he remembered feeling. Others experience similar thrills. Britt Arnesen (2001), a biology student at the University of Alaska working on an archaeological field project, writes in her journal, after making her first find,

Discoveries at Monte Polizzo

Discoveries listed by the participants of the archaeological project working at Monte Polizzo on the Mediterranean island of Sicily in 1999 and 2000 (cf. Holtorf forthcoming), based on questionnaire answers to the question, "What was your best find?"

Identified a pit
Ivory pins
A stone axe
A stamp
A wall on the "Acropolis" after one
    week of deturfing
A site found while surveying
A fireplace
A small pot
A kind of brick, which we hadn't found
    before
An entire pot in situ
An almond tree with wonderful
    almonds on it
Dente di Lupo sherds
A fruit stone while flotating
Two very coarse pot sherds carefully
    wrapped up in a large piece of cotton
Fitting the pieces together of a big
    pithos; it was great to see the vessel
A crushed pot, which was my first find
    ever
An intact pot
Iron Age sherds
Roman fineware
A vessel with an anthropomorphic
    handle
A pyxis lid
Two brooches
Roman pottery of different sorts
A bronze fibula
A bronze bead and a weight

Some pieces of worked black ceramics
Whilst sherd washing, I found that
    under the dirt were decorations
Fragments of ceramics from eastern
    Greece
A peculiar kind of mineral
The remains of a well-preserved pithos
Many pieces of ceramics, metal, and
    animal bone
A wall
Bedrock outside the wall of Building A
The first loom weight we found
Proven right that a wall was actually a
    rubble collapse
Iron fragments
A horse figurine
A ceramic vase
10 well preserved Bronze Age pots
Two separate single burials
A mass grave of about seven individuals
A fragment of a Bronze lance
A fossilized bug
A nice Greek imported pot
A little Greek vase was whole and in
    situ and turned out to be decorated
The first pieces of pottery we found
The rediscovery of a previously
    excavated site
Two porcupines I found on the ground
Pottery vessels that are whole and
    abundant

and there it was. The clearest obsidian that I had thought only existed in the memories of tired academics and dry textbooks. A loud victory cry rang out over the Koyukuk Valley. . . . I am high. I am goofy and high. . . . This is the first site I have ever found. . . . I will always know that it is there, with clues to the mystery of human origins. . . . What a feeling this is!

To me, these are examples of how archaeologists generally feel about making discoveries but are often not honest enough to mention in their writings. Archaeological discoveries are as material as they are abstract, and it is this material dimension that matters so much. In a certain sense, excavating is also about finding oneself, both as a professional and as an embodied individual, hoping to experience personal satisfaction and peer recognition by finding things.

Finding Yourself

Digging provides access to yourself. By that I do not necessarily mean a dissection of the body, although this particular kind of digging emerged at the same time as both geology and archaeology began their own quests into the deep (see Ebeling 2004; Thomas 2004: 150–54, 158). More importantly, digging also allows access to oneself in a metaphorical way.

On archaeological excavations diggers commonly reflect and converse about their individual backgrounds and personal beliefs, as well as about their respective hopes and aims for the future. In this way, the physical activity of digging itself becomes cathartic, causing diggers to reflect upon their lives, identities, and personalities in interaction with others (e.g., Arnesen 2001). Oral history projects can yield a similar effect. One oral history manual, which encouraged workers to find themselves by investigating the history of their own workplaces and to challenge the existing dominant narratives, was given the fitting title *Dig Where You Stand* (Lindqvist 1978). Social historian Paul Thompson has argued that oral history can render people an invaluable service. By going back over their lives, people develop confidence in their own accounts of the past and in their own speech, often gaining dignity, strength, and a sense of purpose (Thompson 1988: 11, 157). In political terms, this outcome can also be seen as a liberation of ordinary people from the experience of being voiceless. Through exploring and communicating their memories, by digging where they stand, the "informants" find out, reaffirm, and express who they are, where they belong, and who they want to be.

Immediate access to the self was also what Sigmund Freud (1856–1939) promised to achieve through psychoanalysis. Significantly, Freud understood psychoanalysis as the "archaeology of the human soul." Under the spell of Heinrich Schliemann's widely publicized archaeological excavations at the Turkish site of Troy and Mycenae in Greece, among other places, Freud excavated deep into people's psyches (figure 2.5). He claimed to reach into the preserved layers of early childhood, making discoveries of amazing treasures (see Kuspit 1989; Mertens and Haubl 1996: 15–24; Wallace 2004: chapter 4). When reading Freud with this archaeological metaphor in mind, the psychoanalysts Ernest Wolf and Sue Nebel (1978) were impressed by the ubiquity of references to prehistory, archaeology, and geology in his entire work (see also chapter 4).

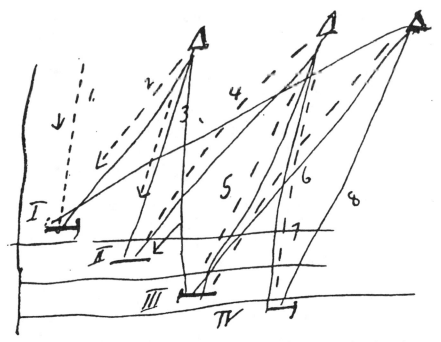

Figure 2.5   Freud's sketch of the analytic work showing penetrations into deeper and deeper layers. Source: S. Freud. 1950. *Aus den Anfängen der Psychoanalyse.* London: Imago, 217.

Applying a similar archaeological metaphor, Casimir, a Tube worker in Tobias Hill's novel *Underground* (1999), explores the passages and shelters of the London Underground. In the process he catches up with his own buried childhood memories from Poland. This passage from near the beginning of the story expresses some of the dynamics of the underground, both literally and metaphorically:

> He remembers his own first few days on the Underground. The feeling of control in the tunnels and halls, their light and air and even life rationed out; and with that, the gradual calm of finding his own life under control. The darkness out in the open, all around him, so that although it could and can still bring him out in a cold sweat, he is always ready for it. . . . Most of all, he remembers the Tube seeming like a hiding place. It felt as if he was coming to ground here, waiting for something to catch up with him. He doesn't know what he is waiting for. (Hill 1999: 8)

It is his own past and his own identity that Casimir is catching up with underground. Academic archaeology too can be instrumental in assisting people with finding themselves. For to know who you are, you need to dig where you stand. Sometimes this is being taken literally. Investigating the past of one's own people, for example, can contribute to building up very strong national identities in the present. Such collective identities, although they have sometimes been linked to chauvinistic attitudes, can provide certainties in an uncertain world. They can even help with resisting and overcoming oppression. Occasionally, archaeology has thus been able to help people to come to grips with a traumatic past.

South African archaeologists in Cape Town, for instance, have been investigating remains in the nineteenth-century suburb of District Six, which in 1966 was declared a "whites only" residential area and subsequently cleared of some sixty thousand inhabitants and their houses (Hall 2001). Redevelopment, however, ran into many problems since District Six had become a rallying point for opposition to the forced removals that were taking place throughout the country. Finally, in 1997, after the end of apartheid, the area was returned to its former residents. What they received was largely an empty field with some religious buildings still standing; mostly mere traces of the former streets, houses, and associated artifacts remained. For the former residents and their descendents, the engagement with the remaining material culture, such as the old street signs, which had miraculously survived, has become a way to deal with and construct their memories of injustice and their identities as dispossessed and dispersed. In 1997 the District Six Museum organized an art festival. One of the artists involved was Igshaan Jacobs, once forcibly removed from the area and now collecting ceramic sherds, like an archaeologist. These sherds have a very personal significance for him: "This porcelain is how I relate to my history. If I could just piece together one small cup from all the pieces I've gathered I would have something to hold onto" (from a newspaper report, cited in Hall 2001: 302).

Another sense in which archaeology has allowed people to find or be themselves is by assisting indigenous populations in postcolonial contexts, e.g., in Australia, to claim the land on which they have been living as their own. Land claims based on archaeological evidence are complex and highly disputed issues, but it is evident that archaeological results can have far-reaching consequences for entire communities. Similarly, the controversial Native American Graves Protection and Repatriation Act of the United States has given indigenous communities control over the dead bodies of their distant ancestors, thus reaffirming their worldviews and identities.

Recovering Truths

People who do not want to be found or found out or to have too much found out about them, such as tramps, secret agents, or terrorists, tend to go underground. Intended secrets must be buried. The underground thus contains significant truths that can be revealed by digging. As Rosalind Williams (1990: 49) puts it, "The assumptions that truth is found by digging, and that the deeper we go the closer we come to absolute truth, have become part of the intellectual air we breathe."

Accordingly, archaeologists are widely perceived as detectives who solve profound mysteries and reveal the secrets of the past (see chapter 4). They are portrayed as the heroes who find hidden treasures, make stones speak, and bring lost civilizations back to life (cf. Cohodas 2003). When the archaeologist turns up, eventually everything will come to light, or so they say in popular culture. The archaeologists themselves are careful these days to avoid the impression that the finds and features they identify can speak for themselves or allow only one correct interpretation of the past. But digging is nevertheless still widely seen as truth seeking, and looking at the find is supposedly to know the truth. Fictional detectives especially tend to employ this approach, whether literally searching for the decisive material clue that reveals the entire truth (the "smoking gun") or metaphorically digging to find out what really happened at the scene of crime. Agatha Christie, who was married to the archaeologist Max Mallowan, lets her detective, Hercule Poirot, describe the latter procedure as his own approach:

> Once I went professionally to an archaeological excavation—and I learned something there. In the course of an excavation, when something comes up out of the ground, everything is cleared away very carefully all around it. You take away the loose earth, and you scrape here and there with a knife until finally your object is there, all alone, ready to be drawn and photographed with no extraneous matter confusing it. That is what I have been seeking to do—clear away the extraneous matter so that we can see the truth—the naked shining truth. (1960: 204)

Similarly, Thompson (1988: 150) writes that oral history could involve "unpick[ing] the layers of memory, dig[ging] back into its darknesses, hoping to reach the hidden truth." A prominent metaphorical archaeologist of more recent times, philosopher Michel Foucault, described his approach in *The Order of Things* (1970) and *The Archaeology of Knowledge* (1992) as "archaeological." As an archaeologist of ideas, Foucault treats a given epoch of intellectual history as an excavation site. He does not want to interpret what appears on the surface but instead tries to describe systematically the underlying configurations of particular discourses (Foucault 1970: xxiii; 1992: 7, 138–40, 206–8). In the view of many, this kind of describing truths found below the surface represents what archaeologists do (Thomas 2004: 149–56).

The Earth as Body

The underground contains not only treasures and truths that we are free to obtain, but it can also be seen as a body with precious organs and a right to physical integrity. The environmental historian Carolyn Merchant (1980: chapter 1) argues that before, in the modern world, the cosmos became a "machine," many cultures considered it to be a sacred organism (see also Eliade 1962: 41–57). Mother Earth provided for her people, both on her surface and in the ground below. Deep inside the fertile ground grew pots, as did minerals and metals (see figure 2.6). Mines were compared to the Earth's vagina, and metallurgy was the hastening of the birth of the living metal in the artificial womb of the furnace, after aborting its normal growth cycle. As far as the pots are concerned, it must have been noted to what extent they resembled the vessels made by the potters of the time, but they were nevertheless taken to grow slowly underground, creating mounds, as if the earth were pregnant. Eventually the pots appeared on the surface, at first soft and fragile, then becoming hard and solid under the powers of sun and air, as scholars observed and discussed from the fifteenth century onwards (Franz 1931). Archaeology has, however, always done more than harvest ripe goods on the surface.

According to Michael Shanks (1992: 68–69), conquering sites and investigating ever-new ancient finds carry strong erotic connotations: "Excavation is striptease. The layers are peeled off slowly; eyes of intent scrutiny. The pleasure is in seeing more." By the same token, the archaeology enthusiast and literary scholar Jennifer Wallace (2004: 81) reports how she was told on a dig that excavation resembles the process of "undressing a woman. . . . It is very exciting gradually uncovering a pot." Moreover, archaeological excavation, like mining, can also be seen as a form of penetration, even rape, of the earth, literally undermining the sacred organism (Zintzen 1998: 331). According to this image, the archaeologist inflicts wounds and injuries on Mother Earth, whose treasures really ought to stay where they are. Similar thinking is prevalent among some environmentalists who seek to protect the originally healthy earth from exploitation and destruction. Modern pagans and some local people have recently argued that the timber circle at Holme-next-the-Sea ("Seahenge") was a sacred place of the land. It ought not to have been "rescued" by archaeological excavation, "like a tooth pulled," leaving an open wound, but respected for its sanctity and protected as it was (Wood 2002: 53).

Archaeology can also be seen as facilitating the birth of additional sites, thus giving new life to what had been lost at some point in the past.

Figure 2.6 The underground as womb and tomb: Alison Lochhead's *Death Within Life* 2. In the opening sequence of Indiana Jones and the Temple of Doom, 1984, Willie says: "Well—I thought archaeologists were always funny little men searching for their mummies." Photographs by Alison Lochhead, reproduced by permission.

The scientist then appears as the consultant or midwife who helps the earth give birth or saves her body from illnesses and heals injuries. The environmental pressure group Friends of the Earth International, for example, according to its mission statement, aims to "protect the earth against further deterioration and repair damage inflicted upon the environment by human activities and negligence" (www.foei.org/about/mission_statement.html, accessed October 4, 2004). They advocate treating the natural world with respect. This vision of caring for a fragile earth can also be made relevant to archaeology (see chapter 8). Indeed, Earthwatch, a different organization, but one likewise focused on earth matters, also supports many archaeological projects. A recent advertisement in *Archaeology* magazine asked, "Can you use a shovel?" and invited "real people" to make "a difference in the world" by joining "exciting field research projects," including archaeological digs. But in archaeological research, as in medicine, there is no final diagnosis unless all the symptoms have been carefully examined, the X-rays have been inspected, and the results of scientifically analyzed samples have arrived. At the same time, there is often a similar sense of urgency in medical and in archaeological rescue operations.

Just as medical doctors may save human bodies from death, archaeologists rescue ancient remains in the ground from imminent destruction, whether by developers or sinking groundwater levels. Archaeological consultants apply their skills by cleanly executing the cuts, carefully removing the ulcers, and fixing any fractures. During the operation the site should be kept clean of dirt. All activities and findings are meticulously recorded for later checks. Various special tools and high-tech devices are used, from toothbrushes and tiny dentist's instruments for the more delicate operations to nonintrusive geophysical measuring instruments and ground-penetrating radar. In the end, the archaeologist is satisfied with the work done, and the wound in the earth is filled and left to heal, but scars will remain visible for some time, if not forever.

In an urban context, below the pavement and normally invisible are the bones, muscles, organs, blood vessels, and nerves of our towns and cities: the many strong supports on which the buildings above physically rest; the electricity cables; the tunnels full of pedestrians, vehicles, and trains; the ventilation shafts; the canalization for sewage, rain water, and even entire rivers; the pipes for gas or water; and the telephone lines, among many other things. You may even find some very large cellars, bunkers, and entire shopping centers below the urban surface (see Macaulay 1976; www.berliner-unterwelten.de, accessed October 4, 2004). Many of these structures were begun or completed during the nineteenth century, effectively bringing mining techniques into the heart of the cities. They are the infrastructure of permanent human occupation and enable human life above to function smoothly. Yet, as with the development of modern medicine, the aspirations of building modern cities were at least as much metaphorical as they were practical: their extensive underground support systems literally undermined the old ways of life and resulted from a wider quest for progress, power, security, and a desire for heroic journeys into new worlds (Williams 1990).

Today, it is as if cities require intensive care. Fluids and currents are pumped in and out at regulated paces, all parameters are closely monitored in control centers, and specialists are on standby for rapid interventions whenever and wherever required. Occasionally, archaeologists are called in to assist. They are asked to document carefully and remove some of the urban organism's dead tissue, long defunct bones, or formerly vital organs. This is considered necessary so that the city can be continuously rebuilt and urban life can keep thriving.

These, then, are some important cultural themes associated with the underground. They give significance to what lies below the surface and how it is recovered and investigated. Such connotations are important because archaeology necessarily evokes them through its own practice and perception. A similar theme is important in this context, too. This theme is not about archaeology's realm of study but about the conduct of archaeological fieldwork.

THE ARCHAEOLOGIST IN THE FIELD

There is a cloud of noxious vapors which follows our group. It is a hybrid stench of destruction born from the ashes of microwaved blood, sweat, and DEET, sometimes a little marijuana smoke, and usually mostly sweat. This is the smell of archaeologists at work.

—Britt Arnesen (2001)

As I have shown in the previous chapter, entering the underground and accessing what lies below the surface can be rewarding in many ways. The aim of digging is to make discoveries and find treasures of various sorts, literally or metaphorically. Archaeology becomes an adventure into the unknown. It is these kinds of meanings of archaeological fieldwork and of making archaeological discoveries that I discuss in this chapter, thus continuing my discussion of the cultural connotations of archaeology.

The Adventure of Archaeological Fieldwork

Fieldwork has always been considered a crucial part of archaeology's identity, both inside and outside the discipline (see DeBoer 1999). Among archaeologists themselves, those who do not do fieldwork are often mocked as "armchair archaeologists." It is therefore not surprising that practical fieldwork is widely considered of central importance for the training of students. As Stephanie Moser (1995: 185) puts it in a study of Australian prehistoric archaeology, "it was in the field that students learnt how to 'do archaeology' and thus become 'real' archaeologists." This emphasis on fieldwork is, however, only partly to do with learning the practical skills of archaeology. In the field students also learn the unspoken rules, values, and traditions of the disciplinary culture of archaeology (Moser forthcoming; Holtorf forthcoming). Moser is therefore right in stating that going into the field can be considered the principal initiation

39

rite for an apprentice archaeologist. Enduring the ordeals of fieldwork tests students' commitment and, in turn, earns them rank and status. Such educational ideals and strategies probably go back much further than the origins of the academic discipline of archaeology in the age of modern nation-states, which have repeatedly gone to war against each other during the nineteenth and twentieth centuries. Military analogies implied in conducting "campaigns" of fieldwork, enduring tough conditions in the "trenches," and enforcing "discipline" on site seem nevertheless to be particularly deeply felt among archaeologists (Lucas 2001a: 8). This is not surprising since a few influential, early archaeologists, such as Gen. Augustus Pitt-Rivers (1827–1900) and Brig. Sir Mortimer Wheeler (1890–1976) in the United Kingdom and Maj. John Powell (1834–1902) in the United States, had military backgrounds.

Archaeological fieldwork has traditionally had strong gendered associations and is often perceived as a masculinist practice. Based on her doctoral research in Australia, Moser (forthcoming) traces archaeology's "masculine" associations back to the important roles played by themes such as the colonial frontier, romantic exploration, the outdoors, action, hardship, strength, and drink. Much of this imagery is taken up in one typical portrayal of the archaeologist in popular culture as a male wearing a khaki safari suit and a pith helmet, possibly carrying a gun (DeBoer 1999). Alfred Kidder (1949: XI) famously argues that

> in popular belief, and unfortunately to some extent in fact, there are two sorts of archaeologists, the hairy-chested and the hairy-chinned. [The hairy-chested variety appears] as a strong-jawed young man in a tropical helmet, pistol on hip, hacking his way through the jungle in search of lost cities and buried treasure. His boots, always highly polished, reach to his knees, presumably for protection against black mambas and other sorts of deadly serpents. The only concession he makes to the difficulties and dangers of his calling is to have his shirt enough unbuttoned to reveal the manliness of his bosom. The hairy-chinned archaeologist . . . is old. He is benevolently absent-minded. His only weapon is a magnifying glass, with which he scrutinizes inscriptions in forgotten languages. Usually his triumphant decipherment coincides, in the last chapter, with the daughter's rescue from savages by the handsome young assistant.

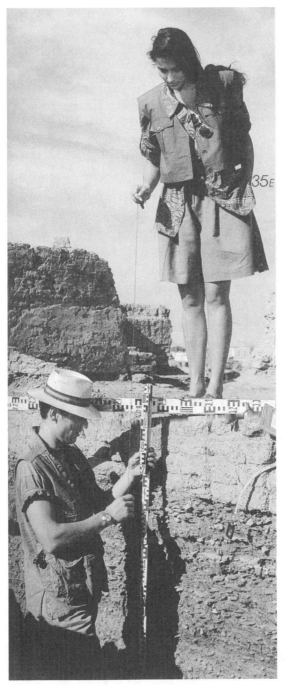

Figure 3.1 Fashion in the "colonial style" worn by "model archaeologists" at an excavation in Egypt. Source: *Verena* no. 5 (1990): 73. Photograph by Wilfried Beege, reproduced by permission.

With this cliché in mind, especially that concerning the hairy-chested archaeologist, the American archaeologist Larry Lahren once called archaeologists "the cowboys of science," living a life of romance and risky adventure. In an article about Lahren himself, he was described as a horse-riding entrepreneur, once known for bar fights and unsuited to academic life but now working for the cause of archaeology (Cahill 1981). Another good example is the field archaeologist Phil Harding of the immensely popular British TV series *Time Team* (see www.channel4.com/history/timeteam). Stephanie Moser, a specialist in representations, describes him in her forthcoming essay as follows: "With his long hair, leather jacket, jeans, hat and strong regional accent, this fieldworker lives up to the popular conception of what it means to be an archaeologist. The cowboy type hat that he wears is of particular significance as a symbol of adventure and exploration."

Arguably, this cliché archaeologist also has an impact on the self-perception of archaeologists, affecting recruitment, specialization, and preferences for certain professional activities. In the past women have sometimes been actively discouraged from going into the field at all. Although much has improved, and female students are now often in the majority in archaeology degree programs, they may occasionally still feel pressure (or a desire) to act more masculine on excavations. By the same token, supposedly feminine activities, such as drawing, can be frowned upon when carried out by male archaeologists (Woodall and Perricone 1981; Zarmati 1995: 46; Gero 1996; Lucas 2001a: 7–9; Moser forthcoming). Likewise, it might be argued that at least some of the fictitious female archaeologists appearing in popular culture, like *Tomb Raider*'s Lara Croft and *Relic Hunter*'s Sydney Fox (see table 3.1), are essentially male characters in female disguises.

Although there are variations to the stereotype, the archaeologist remains clearly recognizable in popular culture, occurring widely in literature and the mass media, including film and TV (see, e.g., Membury 2002; M. Russell 2002). According to David Day's survey of TV archaeology (1997: 3), there are almost 140 different films and videos that feature archaeologists. In recent years, the computer games of the *Tomb Raider* series (figure 3.2) have been particularly influential. *Tomb Raider* is the most popular archaeology-inspired interactive entertainment series released thus far. With total sales of the action games reaching twenty-

Table 3.1 Some Major Archaeologists of Popular Culture

Archaeologist		URL
Dr. Cornelius	A chimpanzee in the film *The Planet of the Apes*	www.movieprop.com/ tvandmovie/PlanetoftheApes
Lara Croft	The heroine of the computer game and *Tomb Raider* films	www.tombraider.com; www.cubeit.com/ctimes
Professor Sydney Fox, historian in the Department of Ancient Studies	The heroine of the TV series *Relic Hunter*	www.relichunter.tk
Melina Havelock, marine archaeologist	Bond girl in *For Your Eyes Only*	www.thegoldengun.co.uk/fyeo/ fyeowomendf.htm
Daniel Jackson, Egyptologist	The hero in the film *Stargate* and subsequent TV series *Stargate SG-1*	www.geocities.com/ eventmovies/stargate.htm; www.stargatesgl.com
Professor Indiana Jones	The hero in novels by various authors and three films by George Lucas and Steven Spielberg	www.theindyexperience.com; www.indianajones.com
Indiana Pipps, Indiana Ding, Indiana Goof, Indiana Jöns, Arizona Goof, etc.	Goofy's cousin who appears in Disney's *Donald Duck* stories under various names in different countries	stp.ling.uu.se/~starback/dcml/ chars/arizona.html
Professor Lucien Kastner, Sir Robert Eversley	Interviewees in the sketch "Archaeology Today" in *Monty Python's Flying Circus*	www.ibras.dk/montypython/ epIsode21.htm
Professor Kilroy, Professor Articus, Dr Charles Lightning	A character with different names in the Lego *Adventurers* theme featuring Johnny Thunder	www.geocities.com/ EnchantedForest/Cottage/ 5900/Adventurers.html
Professor Fujitaka Kinomoto (Aiden Avalon)	Character in the originally Japanese anime *Cardcaptor Sakura*	sakura.prettysenshi.com
Dr. Eric Leidner	The murderer in Agatha Christie's *Murder in Mesopotamia* (1936)	www.agathachristie.com/ booksplays/bookpages/ 1961.shtml
Lintilla	A clone in Douglas Adam's radio play *The Hitchhiker's Guide to the Galaxy 2* (1980)	www.thelogbook.com/ b5covers/hhg/year2.htm
Professor William Harper Littlejohn	A character in the 1930s/1940s *Doc Savage* novels by Lester Dent (and other associated comics, radio shows, and a movie from 1975)	members.aol.com/the86floor; members.netvalue.net/ robsmalley

(continues)

Table 3.1   Continued

Archaeologist		URL
Martin Mystère	The hero in an Italian comic series	www.bvzm.com
Evelyn O'Connell (Carnarvon), Jonathan Carvnarvon, Egyptologists	Major characters in the *Mummy* films and recent computer games	www.themummy.com
Amelia Peabody and Radcliff Emerson, Egyptologists	Main characters in a series of novels by Elizabeth Peters	www.mpmbooks.com/Amelia
Jean-Luc Picard, captain of the Enterprise; Professor Richard Galen; Vash; Lieutenant Marla Aster; Professor Robert Crater	Various characters in the TV series *Star Trek* and associated fiction	www.startrek.com
Will Rock	The hero of a computer game	www.will-rock.com
Professor Robson	The "hunky" professor in the soft-porn film series *The Adventures of Justine* (1995–1996)	rarevideos.bravepages.com/justine.htm
Professor Bernice Summerfield	The heroine of several novels by various authors, originally part of *Doctor Who*	www.bernicesummerfield.co.uk
Professor Hercules Taragon, Americanist	A character in two *Tintin* adventures	www.tintin.com
Miss Wood	A character in *The King's Dragon* story of the children's TV series *Look and Read*	www.lookandread.fsnet.co.uk/stories/king

All URLs were correct on October 1, 2004.

five million units worldwide, each game has topped the PlayStation game best-seller lists. The subsequent feature film grossed more than U.S. $60 million from sales in its first week alone (Watrall 2002: 164). This astounding popularity implies that Lara Croft has an enormous influence on public perceptions of archaeology. The slightly older Indiana Jones movies of the 1980s have arguably been even more influential.

Featuring the archaeologist as a popular stereotype, the archaeological romance of eerie adventures involving exotic locations, treasure hunting, and fighting for a good cause has become a widely used theme in popular culture. Whether deliberately created as such or not, such stereotypes now

Figure 3.2 Lara Croft in Cambridge, United Kingdom. Photograph by Cornelius Holtorf, 2002.

occur in a wide range of popular-culture products and venues, including the following, among others:

- Movies (Day 1997; M. Russell 2002; see also us.imdb.com/search—search for "archaeologist" in "plots")

- TV documentaries and series (Norman 1983; L. Russell 2002)

- Literary fiction (Korte 2000; e.g., Rollins 2000)

- Magazines (Ascher 1960; Gero and Root 1990)

- Advertisements (figure 3.1; Talalay forthcoming)

- Comics (Service 1998a)

- Computer games (figure 3.2; Watrall 2002)

CHAPTER 3

- Toys (figure 3.3; M. Russell 2002: 51–52; e.g., Knight 1999)

- Theme parks and casino-hotels (see chapter 8; Malamud 2001)

The Hardships and Dangers of Fieldwork

Entering the underground is under any circumstances risky and dangerous. This holds true for miners and cavers as much as it does for volcanol-
ogists. You never know what is hiding in the darkness, and if you
encounter something unpleasant or downright deadly, you cannot rely on
making it back to the surface in time; you may even end up deeper still.
The underground is full of unexpected surprises and unknown hazards,
causing irrational fears. He who searches for treasures and brings light to
where there was darkness must be willing to compromise safety and prepared to experience some pain. James Bond, for example, knows how dangerous it can be to enter the operation bases of his evil enemies, which are
often, not coincidentally, located underground. These spaces contain both
a lot of mighty weaponry and ruthless mercenaries who know how to use
them. They also tend to contain some kind of superweapon, which threat-
ens all humankind but requires both special expertise to be put to action
and James Bond to be put out of action. The theme is old: in folklore
mighty treasures are invariably protected by powerful superhuman security
guards against whom we humans are mostly helpless. This is where risks
and dangers meet their counterparts of control and protection. Both are
two sides of the same coin. Subterranean military or political headquarters
in deeply buried bunkers can so become spaces not only of great threat
and danger for those outside but also of ultimate security and safety for
those inside (see Williams 1990: chapter 7).

The archaeologist is generally the person who is, at least at first, not
inside but outside such fortresses. Moreover, the archaeologist is frequently subjected to all sorts of threats to limb and life when attempting
to get in. One great example for this image of archaeological fieldwork is
James Rollins's novel *Excavation* (2000), describing the discoveries and
ordeals of a group of archaeology students in the Peruvian jungle. The
text on the back cover reads as follows:

> The South American jungle guards many secrets and a remarkable site
> nestled between two towering Andean peaks, hidden from human eyes

Urban Explorers

Contemporary urban explorers are the archaeologists of the modern city. Although cities are human made, for those living in them it can still be exciting and adventurous to explore the seemingly uncharted areas below the city's surfaces. These explorers are often well organized and publish detailed advice and reports about their explorations of abandoned factories, hotels, office buildings, tunnels, and drains, among other sites (e.g., Predator 1999; infiltration.org). One experienced explorer, who claims to "have done 147 drains in 6 Australian states, in addition to numerous rail tunnels, bridge rooms, abandoned bunkers and other concealed underground places," explains the fascination of this hobby:

> In life, you make choices. You can stay in bed and take no risks, or you can go out and get a life. This involves the taking of risks, telling of yarns, breaking of silly laws which restrict your freedom, finding out things of an unusual or interesting nature. Now, some people take drugs, some people watch TV, some people drive cars faster than the posted speed limit, some people get heavily into teletubbies, some people play golf. Since we find these things not very interesting, we explore drains. We like the dark, the wet, humid, earthy smell. We like the varying architecture. We like the solitude. We like the acoustics, the wildlife, the things we find, the places we come up, the comments on the walls, the maze-like quality; the sneaky, sly subversiveness of being under a heavily-guarded Naval Supply base or under the Justice and Police Museum. . . . We like the controlled nature of the risks involved. We like the timelessness of a century-old tunnel, the darkness yawning before us, saying "Come, you know not what I hide within me." (Predator 1999)

A few years ago I participated in an international excavation project on Monte Polizzo on Sicily in southern Italy. I remember that one of the most exciting places to explore for many of the fifty plus project members was the deserted bottom floor of the building in whose first and second floors we were accommodated. This large space was once used as a clinic, and it had obviously not been cleaned up since its closure, only blocked off with bricks in a rudimentary fashion insufficient to stop us entering and exploring. We found a mess. One room was full of medical apparatus and papers spread out on the floor. In the center stood what looked like an X-ray machine; elsewhere were an old Italian flag, a plough that was possibly still being used occasionally and accessed through a locked gate, broken glass, and other rubbish spread out all around. One room full of sewage smelled appallingly. We loved it.

for thousands of years. Dig deeper through layers of rock and mystery, through centuries of dark, forgotten legend. Into ancient catacombs where ingenious traps have been laid to ensnare the careless and unsuspecting; where earth-shattering discoveries—and wealth beyond imagining—could be the reward for those with the courage to face the terrible unknown. Something is waiting here where the perilous journey ends, in the cold, shrouded heart of a breathtaking necropolis; something created by Man, yet not humanly possible. Something wondrous. Something terrifying. (Rollins 2000)

This will sound very familiar in the light of the previous chapter's discussion. A secret and hidden site of the past can be reached by digging deeper; it promises earth-shattering discoveries and wealth beyond imagining, but the journey is, of course, also fraught with dangers.

Real excavations can be tough, too. The excavations on Monte Polizzo (Sicily) involved exhausting physical work on a mountaintop and a lot of sweating in the merciless Mediterranean summer sun. To compensate (and reward?) ourselves we drank all sorts of alcoholic drinks in the evenings and enjoyed visits to beautiful beaches on the weekends. An archaeological life of exhaustion and earned rewards (Holtorf forthcoming). Elsewhere, it is the cold climatic conditions that can make archaeology a tough occupation; for example in Alaska:

The advertisements for the Peace Corps say: "the toughest job you'll ever love" but it's clear to me that these people have never tried archaeological survey in the interior of Alaska. In the early morning we crossed a thicket of alders and everyone disappeared into the jungle. Only our voices could guide us through the rain. (Arnesen 2001)

Even when the geographical location and context is less exotic, as in urban archaeology, much tends to be made of those aspects of the project that retain at least some degree of adventure and earned rewards: the difficulties of interpreting a complex site, the bad weather, the mounting time pressure. Stories about the hardship of archaeological fieldwork and anecdotes about students or colleagues that derive from a shared experience of being in the field are generally a popular subject of conversation also among the

Thesis 4:
Archaeological fieldwork is about making discoveries under tough conditions in exotic locations.

archaeologists themselves. Sometimes in such discussions I recall some of my more extraordinary excavation experiences in 1991 and 1992 in Georgia.

We flew to Tbilisi via Moscow, only two weeks after the attempted putsch and right in the middle of a civil war in Georgia. Our excavation site was far removed in the east of the country and fairly safe. But one weekend we arrived in the capital, Tbilisi, and could sense a strange atmosphere literally hanging over the town. That night, the town center had experienced violent clashes between supporters of the two sides. We saw people with arms, buses being used as roadblocks, and tanks moving outside the parliament building. Back on the excavation, some of our elderly workmen proposed toasts to the unforgotten Stalin. When we returned a year later for the second excavation season, the Soviet Union had ceased to exist and a new government had taken over in Georgia. Bullet holes and burned-out floors marked the buildings of Tbilisi. During both years, we could sense how much our hosts' attention was distracted from the archaeological site we excavated. But as guests we were told very little about what was really going on so that we had to rely on BBC World Service broadcasts to follow the events in our host country. Occasionally we Westerners were the honorary guests at local gatherings, but we never quite knew which of the political sides we served by lending them prestige and status in a bloody conflict. The day before we left, the local archaeologist we were staying with drove two of us through Tbilisi to visit a friend. After several checks at armed control posts, we reached a police station where the friend turned out to be one of the policemen on duty. Being a good host, he showed us the cells of his station, complete with their occupants. It became even more bizarre (and memorable) when we were offered live ammunition from his pistol as souvenirs since this was all he could offer under the circumstances. Contrary to my expectations, but relying on good local advice, I easily managed to smuggle my cartridge through the X-ray machine at the airport, and I have still got it.

Risks and dangers exist also on the metaphorical level. Casimir, the underground worker in Tobias Hill's novel *Underground* (1999), for example, has got some reservations about the underground that turn out to be literal as well as metaphorical:

> What disturbs him is what the Underground will do to people. It is
> where Casimir has come to ground, but he knows it can be an unsafe

hiding place. Things are less mundane down here, more precarious. There is always the way the Underground can contain things, trapping them in its corners, hiding them, making them stronger. (p. 45)

Psychoanalytic treatment, too, may yield all sorts of frightening insights into a patient's psyche and should therefore not be taken lightly. But for Freud even the adventurous aspects of archaeological fieldwork were part of his archaeological metaphor:

> The narcissistic glory of Schliemann was meant to make the labor of remembering easier for the neurotic person. Everybody could secretly feel like a famous archaeologist. The strains of the excavation were comparable to the displeasure that set in when confronted with inhibitions to tell everything. If Heinrich Schliemann worked in the open in any weather, the patient too was not to shy away from every effort to dedicate him- or herself eagerly to Freud's method of free association and thus to uncover his or her memory layer by layer. (Mertens and Haubl 1996: 18–19; my translation[1])

Another kind of danger emanates not from what lies underground but from the explorers themselves. They can be responsible for various negative consequences, which the innocent, local people have to suffer as a result of their "lost" worlds being "explored," their "mysterious" "treasures" "discovered," and generally their "secrets" "revealed" (Cohodas 2003). Revealing secret truths undoes the status quo and causes change, not just in Western academia and for the explorers concerned but also at the sites of discovery. For example, internal conflicts may arise or additional outsiders may arrive and seek to exploit what archaeologists have revealed. In accounts of archaeological adventures, such consequences are often only retrospectively considered and regretted, when it is already too late. This more sinister side of archaeology, which in part draws on the

---

1. Original German text: "Der narzißtische Ruhm Schliemanns sollte dem neurotischen Menschen die Arbeit an der Erinnerung verschönen. Jeder konnte sich insgeheim wie ein berühmter Archäologe fühlen, und die Strapazen der Ausgrabung waren der Unlust vergleichbar, die sich angesichts von Widerständen, alles zu erzählen, einstellten. Wenn Heinrich Schliemann bei jedem Wetter auf freiem Feld arbeitete, dann durfte der Patient keine Mühe scheuen, um sich der von Freud entwickelten Methode der freien Assoziation eifrig zu widmen und Schicht für Schicht in der Erinnerung freizulegen."

uncompromising practices of some real explorers of the past, comes to the fore in archaeologists' occasional portrayal as unscrupulous, colonialist treasure hunters who have initially no consideration for any of the upheaval they cause (see figure 3.3). In this vein, Miles Russell writes,

> Archaeologists are the villains. They are tampering with forces that they do not understand. They are the people who raid the tomb, irrespective of the wishes and warnings of the local or indigenous population, awaken the dead, activate the curse, and bring down some immense supernatural nasty upon the world. (2002: 46)

The "curse of the mummy" is a good example of a legendary force of good protecting the legitimate interests of the people who buried the mummy for eternity. First popular after Howard Carter's discovery of the grave of Tutankhamun in 1922 and the subsequent death of Lord Carnarvon, his colleague and sponsor, the curse has remained a key element of the image of archaeology in popular culture until the present day. Since the 1920s cursed Egyptian tombs have recurred frequently in all sorts of genres of literature as well as in many films and even blockbuster movies like *The Mummy* (see Frayling 1992; M. Russell 2002). If archaeologists can bring the past to life and reveal its secrets in the manner of saviors or magicians, there is always a risk, then, that the wrong forces will be unleashed. These are the powers they can no longer control, which threaten their survival and that of their associates, and which demonstrate the ultimate powerlessness of the archaeologists in the face of the mightiness of past civilizations.

Other dangers that may come from the archaeologists' work relate to the way in which their work can be used in unstable political contexts (see Layton et al. 2001). An excavation site and its associated material culture may serve, whether intended by the archaeologists or not, as building blocks for modern nationalism and chauvinistic myths, usually by drawing on ancient glories or presumed long-term continuities (see Silberman 1995; Schmidt and Halle 1999). Ultimately such perceived historical foundations can even provide reasons and justification for wars. In the 1991 Gulf War, both sides used archaeology in their propaganda: whereas Saddam Hussein associated himself with ancient rulers like Sargon the Great, Hammurabi, and Nebuchadnezzar, the U.S.-led allies legitimized

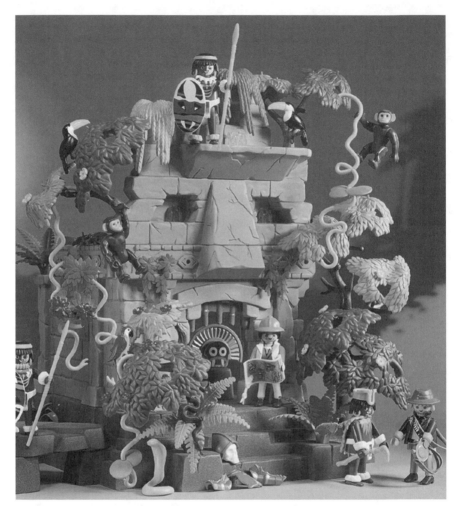

Figure 3.3 Playmobil archaeologists in action: "Two explorers tiptoe softly through the jungle in search of the System X jungle ruin, passing exotic creatures like toucans, parrots, chimpanzees, and dangerous poisonous snakes. They are in search of the ancient mummy and legendary jewels hidden in the eyes of the ruin's rock face. Through the thick underbrush—there it is! Quietly now, or the three native guards might hear. Others have tried to enter before, but a skull with armor at the foot of the stairs tells the story of how they failed. Our explorers manage to sneak by, just in time to reach the dungeon before the push-button gate closes. At last, the mummy! But where is the secret hiding place of the jewels? There's no time to look now, they will have to return later. Good thing they have a map to find their way back through the dense trees, bushes, and hanging plants" (from www.playmobil.de, product description for pack no. 3015, accessed 26 May 2002). Image courtesy of Playmobil, a registered trademark of geobra Brandstätter GmbH & Co. KG, reproduced by permission. The company also holds all rights to the displayed toy figures.

their efforts by claiming to protect "our common heritage" in "the cradle of civilization" from barbarians like Saddam (Pollock and Lutz 1994). A similar picture emerged once again during the war against Iraq in 2003.

Despite such dangers, people often feel compelled to reach below the surface or to observe others in their endeavors underground. Such quests for discovery are epitomized by the figure of the archaeologist doing fieldwork. Yet, archaeological discoveries are not merely appealing as the act of finding treasure below the surface, but also as a process of searching, encountering and categorizing. It is for this reason that archaeological discovery stories are often particularly exciting.

Archaeological Discovery Stories

The feeling of discovering something that bridges the seemingly unfathomable abyss between past and present continues to stir the popular imagination (Zintzen 1998: 138; cf. figure 1.3). It also reinforces the notion that seeking and making finds is a central component of archaeology, which contains "within itself that longing for the unforeseen, that passion for investigation and desire for discovery, which represent the basic motivation of true archaeological activity" (Pallottino 1968: 70). In all these stories, the inevitable climax is the moment of the great discovery, which comes unexpectedly and is in many instances made by complete outsiders. After the hardships of digging, finding treasure is the greatest moment of the archaeologist and a very emotional event. The most famous of these moments, which has often been staged in popular films, was Howard Carter's opening of Tutankhamun's tomb in the Egyptian Valley of the Kings on November 26, 1922. In an often-cited passage, he describes the events as follows:

> The day following (November 26th) was the day of days, the most wonderful that I have ever lived through, and certainly one whose like I can never hope to see again. . . . Slowly, desperately slowly it seemed to us as we watched, the remains of passage debris that encumbered the lower part of the doorway were removed, until at last we had the whole door clear before us. The decisive moment had arrived. With trembling hands I made a tiny breach in the upper left-hand corner. . . . Candle tests were applied as a precaution against possible foul gases, and then,

widening the hole a little, I inserted the candle and peered in, Lord
Carnarvon, Lady Evelyn and Callender standing anxiously beside me to
hear the verdict. At first I could see nothing, the hot air escaping from
the chamber causing the candle flame to flicker, but presently, as my
eyes grew accustomed to the light, details of the room within emerged
slowly from the mist, strange animals, statues, and gold—everywhere
the glint of gold. For the moment—an eternity it must have seemed to
the others standing by—I was struck dumb with amazement, and when
Lord Carnarvon, unable to stand the suspense any longer, inquired anxiously, "Can you see anything?" it was all I could do to get out the words,
"Yes, wonderful things." (cited in Frayling 1992: 104–105)

This is where the fascination of archaeology lies for many (cf. Ascher
1960). Agatha Christie, for example, who often accompanied her husband
Max Mallowan on his excavations in the Near East (see Christie 1977;
Trümpler 2001), found discovering artifacts irresistible indeed: "The lure
of the past came up to grab me. To see a dagger slowly appearing, with its
gold glint, through the sand was romantic. The carefulness of lifting pots
and objects from the soil filled me with a longing to be an archaeologist
myself." (Christie 1977: 377)

This sense of wonder is provided for children visiting Francis Pryor's
excavation site at Flag Fen in eastern England. The facilities include a
sand pit where children are invited to dig for themselves and find their
own (previously prepared) treasures that simulate archaeological finds
(figure 3.4). I saw a similar attraction in a gift shop at Caesars Palace in
Las Vegas, with the main difference that the children were invited to buy
the wonderful things they had discovered in the sand. All this resembles
somewhat the staged excavations that have been organized since the eighteenth century for dignitaries visiting Pompeii: "A freshly discovered edi-
fice which had been thoughtfully filled with coins or statuary was simply
re-buried in order to be discovered once more, with well-rehearsed cries
of surprise, in the honored guest's presence." (Leppmann 1966: 86)

This has been practiced in Germany, too. Reportedly, during the late
nineteenth century, the German royal family and members of their house-
hold used to visit the Saalburg, a well-known excavation site of a Roman
castle. On some of these occasions, finds made of chocolate were hidden
in the ground. They dissolved quickly when the fortunate finder cleaned

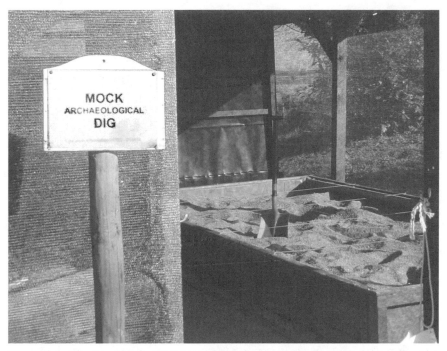

Figure 3.4   Finding wonderful things. All is prepared for the Mock Archaeological Dig at Flag Fen near Peterborough, England. Photograph by Cornelius Holtorf, 2001.

her discovery with water, much to the amusement of the onlookers (Löhlein 2003: 659).

Making archaeological discoveries is a literary theme that has also often been employed to tell the stories both of archaeologists' lives and of the history of archaeology. In this perspective, the archaeologist is a passionate and totally devoted adventurer and explorer who conquers ancient sites and artifacts, thereby pushing forward the frontiers of our knowledge about the past. The associated narratives resemble those of the stereotypical hero who embarks on a quest to which he is fully devoted, is tested in the field, makes a spectacular discovery, and finally emerges as the virtuous man (or, exceptionally, woman) when the quest is fulfilled (see Zarmati 1995: 44; Cohodas 2003).

Best-selling accounts of archaeological romances involving mystery, adventure, and hardship and concluding with the reward of treasure were pioneered by the author Kurt W. Marek, alias C. W. Ceram, who published in 1949 his instant classic *Götter, Gräber und Gelehrte* ("Gods, Graves, and Scholars"). This book tells the story of the "great" archaeological discoveries in the eastern Mediterranean, Egypt, the Middle East, and Central America by focusing on the archaeologists themselves. Prominently included are accounts of the lives and archaeological accomplishments of Heinrich Schliemann (Troy and Mycenae), Arthur Evans (Knossos), Jean-François Champollion (Egyptian hieroglyphics), William Petrie (Egyptian pyramids), Howard Carter (Tutankhamun's tomb), Henry Layard (Nimrud), Leonard Woolley (Ur), Hernando Cortés (Tenochtitlan), and Edward Thompson (Chichén Itzá), among others. The book has by now been translated into thirty languages (including English) and has sold almost five million copies worldwide (Oels 2002). The success of Ceram's writing lies in a mixture of facts and exciting storytelling where readers suffer with their heroes until their eventual success. The use of numerous historical details and the frequent allusions to archaeology, continuously advancing our knowledge by deciphering more and more of the past, became key elements of a new literary genre thus established, the *archäologischer Tatsachenroman*, or fact-based archaeological fiction (Schörken 1995: 71–81). This genre was very successfully continued by others. The Danish archaeologist Geoffrey Bibby (1957) extended the chronological and geographical scope, reporting about prehistoric sites north of the Mediterranean. The German journalist Rudolf Pörtner popularized in several best-selling volumes archaeological discoveries and emerging insights into the prehistory and history of Germany (e.g., Pörtner 1959). Later, another German journalist, Philipp Vandenberg, successfully told (and retold) the stories and discoveries of archaeologists in Greece, Egypt, and the Middle East (e.g., Vandenberg 1977).

An often-used template for any such narrative has been the life and career of Heinrich Schliemann. Like few others, he personified the "lonely" hero who, despite being an outsider, knows "the truth"—in this case about the historical reality of Homer's Troy—early on but is ridiculed until he finally embarks on his quest alone and under great difficulty. In the end, however, Schliemann and the archetypical hero prove themselves right by making great discoveries, becoming accepted as scholars, and being celebrated as national heroes. Many have since drawn inspiration and motivation from this truly mythical story in the history of science (see chapter 2). Even the German emperor Wilhelm II (1859–1941) was knowingly inspired by Heinrich Schliemann's successes. Since 1911 he conducted regular excavations on the Greek island of Corfu and invited Wilhelm Dörpfeld, Schliemann's former collaborator and successor in Troy, to join him not only during the excavations but also on his yacht cruises between the islands, using Homer's *Odyssey* as his travel guide (Löhlein 2003). Wilhelm and countless other amateur researchers, following after Schliemann, exemplify the insight that heroes are not made by their deeds alone but mostly by the stories that are told about their achievements (Zarmati 1995: 44). They all have kept telling themselves heroic stories about archaeologists, while at the same time being keen to tell similar stories about themselves.

One aspect sometimes forgotten in these hero stories is their final element: the eventual downfall of the hero and his being cut down to size. Even the glory of Schliemann began to fade after his death, when questions were raised about the ownership of the artifacts he shipped out of their countries of origin and when it became clear to what extent he had fabricated even his own autobiography (see Zintzen 1998: 271–72). Likewise, Indiana Jones, in *Indiana Jones and the Last Crusade*, manages to get hold of the Holy Grail and save his father, but in the end he cannot hold on to it and remains an ordinary mortal.

The Act of Discovery in Archaeological Practice and Theory

But what about discoveries on modern excavations? How do they fit into the picture? In order to answer this, I first need to say a bit about the dominant understanding of archaeological finds and features as part of the "archaeological record" (Patrick 1985). This record has supposedly been formed by everything left behind from the past on a given site. All excavators need to do in the field is document this record, and for its interpretation the archaeologist simply needs to apply his or her expertise and competently read this documentation, thus the archaeological record itself. This scenario not only does an injustice to the creative tasks of recording and interpreting archaeological material, it also plays down the active role of the excavator in "making" a discovery in the first place, thus maintaining the illusion of an "objectivity" of archaeological facts (see Edgeworth 1990; 2003: 6). In much conventional science, the act of discovering data is indeed considered irrelevant compared to the act of its validation as part of a particular hypothesis. As far as archaeology is concerned, this view is naive (Lucas 2001b: 40).

The British field archaeologist Matthew Edgeworth suggested that to the same extent that theory and writing are kinds of archaeological practice, digging is also a kind of archaeological theory. He made the important observation that, for the most part, emerging objects are anticipated and, therefore, to a certain extent already known before they have actually been found. In this sense, archaeologists have perhaps only ever been able to find what they knew already and were thus able to see and to make sense of (Rehork 1987). Edgeworth found that excavators tend to describe the moment of discovery as the "popping out" or "leaping out" of the find from the soil being worked. They are instantly recognized due to socially shared cognitive schemes of what a particular kind of artifact looks like and where it might be found. For example, Edgeworth tells a story from an excavation of a Bronze Age cemetery on which one would normally expect to find arrowheads, but after six weeks still none had been found. Eventually, however, an arrowhead was found. When the excavator was asked what had first drawn her attention to it, she said, "There was something about the sheen of it . . . it seemed to fall out of the earth nicely." She had recognized it immediately as a worked flint and realized that it was an arrowhead when picking it up (Edgeworth 2003: 55). In cases such as this, the object not only suddenly emerges to catch the excavator's attention and almost pulls her towards it, but at the same time the excavator's anticipatory schemes also leap out to grasp or apprehend the object, both conceptually and physically (Edgeworth 1990: 246; 2003: chapter 7).

After Edgeworth's work from the early 1990s, the act of archaeological discovery was not studied much until recently. The social anthropologist Thomas Yarrow (2003) conducted an ethnographic study of an archaeological excavation, looking in particular at the relationship between the subjectivities of the excavators and the objectivity of the site and its artifacts. He came to the conclusion that finds are "made" into objective "discoveries" by excavators acting objectively, i.e., in correspondence with the collective knowledge and the intellectual and bodily conventions of the discipline. Similarly, the archaeologist Gavin Lucas (2001b) proposed to consider archaeological fieldwork as a materializing practice. He argued that by digging up objects that become "discovered" finds or features, they are being materialized as something they had never

Figure 3.5 Archaeologist doing fieldwork. Use of this image permitted as a licensor of Corel. All rights reserved by Corel.

been before: archaeological data. According to studies such as these, archaeology is not just disinterested observation, but an "encounter" with and transformation of material objects (see also Gero 1996; Lucas 2001a: 16–17; Pearson and Shanks 2001). Part of this encounter is the same sense of wonder that both fictional and nonfictional archaeologists cherish so much.

In both this and the previous chapters I have pointed to the cultural significance of two aspects of archaeology that are normally taken for granted and overlooked in many accounts of the discipline. The underground is a very rich cultural field, and every archaeological work that involves digging has to be seen in relation to it. Similarly, archaeological fieldwork is more than the sum of practicalities; it is an experience that is significant in several ways other than what it purports to be. It is also an adventure that is full of hardship but that eventually leads to wonderful discoveries. These dimensions belong to the materiality of archaeology itself.

But where does this leave the materiality of the past? What precisely is the archaeological value over and above the sense of wonder emanating from artifacts recovered underground by archaeologists in the field? For the most part, they are, of course, traces of past human activities. That brings me to my next chapter.

CHAPTER FOUR
INTERPRETING TRACES

Artefacts mean nothing. It is only when they are interpreted through practice that they become invested with meanings

—John Barrett (1994: 168)

D iscovering material evidence in the present, which is then used to reconstruct events of the past, links detective novels, criminology, and Freud's psychoanalysis with archaeology. Traces are taken as clues for the events that caused them. This chapter discusses this particular interpretation of material culture and how subtly contemporary artists and others have challenged it. These critics suggest that all material culture can be interpreted in many different ways. Its characterization as "clues" for understanding past human action is not at all self-evident but the outcome of very particular interpretations of the context and origin of (certain) things. In the end, the process of reading clues as such may be more important than what is actually understood.

The Archaeologist as Detective—The Detective as Archaeologist

It has often been argued that the archaeologist works like a detective. Massimo Pallottino (1968: 12), for example, describes this similarity in the following way:

> If we were to compare the reconstruction of the past with a large-scale police inquiry or a trial, tradition would be the equivalent to the depositions of the witnesses, and archaeological data would represent the material evidence: the former eloquent and circumstantial, but not always reliable; the latter fragmentary, not always clear in meaning, but in themselves incontrovertible. In the hunt for clues, in the ingenuity required to fit them into place, in the effort to interpret them logically,

archaeologists do in fact very closely resemble criminal investigators. They operate on the front line of historical research like true detectives of the past.

Both archaeology and criminology draw on seemingly incontrovertible material evidence, which is taken to provide significant clues as to what has really gone on. These clues are often provided by telltale traces left on the site. As anything might be significant, comprehensive documentation is of the utmost importance (see Pearson and Shanks 2001: 59–64). Archaeologists are trained and experienced in recording, studying, and interpreting such traces and routinely integrate the results of expert analysis. A wonderful recent example is the continuing analysis of the Ice Man and his equipment, found in 1991 in the Italian Alps and initially handled as a criminal investigation. New evidence regarding this unique, over-five-thousand-year-old find is still coming to light and is always widely reported in the media. The recent discovery of an arrowhead in his body suggests that we are indeed looking at a murder case. On the Discovery Channel's Ice Man Web pages (dsc.discovery.com/convergence/iceman/iceman.html, accessed October 4, 2004) you are even invited to search for clues yourself, come up with your own conclusions, and vote for your favorite death theory.

The archaeologist is thus the detective of the past. Like the detective the archaeologist solves mysteries and is often portrayed as creating light where there was darkness by finding clues and revealing truths (e.g., Ceram 1980; Traxler 1983; Knight 1999; cf. Schörken 1995: 74–75, 82). Both archaeology and criminology did indeed develop parallelly to each other during the second half of the nineteenth century. The genre of the detective novel, too, emerged at that time, and works in this genre have ever since frequently alluded to archaeology (see Neuhaus 2001). One of the most prominent examples for an archaeological detective story is Agatha Christie's *Murder in Mesopotamia* (1994 [1936]), which is set on an excavation based on Leonard Woolley's project in Ur in modern Iraq. Christie saw archaeology as a puzzle about the past and occasionally mentioned in conversations that there were obvious parallels between the work of archaeologists and that of detectives (Joan Oates, personal communication). Hercule Poirot is obviously inspired by archaeological methodology. For instance, at the end of his adventures in Mesopotamia, the archaeologist Dr. Leidner, after having been found out as the murderer, commends the famous detective with the words, "You would have made a good archaeologist, M. Poirot. You have the gift of re-creating the past" (Christie 1937: 215). The detective Poirot thus becomes the archaeologist of a crime. Some archaeologists like Stanley Casson, Glyn Daniel, and Gordon Willey have also written detective novels themselves (Thomas 1976).

> **Thesis 5:**
> The archaeologist is a detective of the past.

Because of such correspondences between detective work and archaeology, it is hardly surprising that the services of archaeologists have occasionally been invaluable to police forces. Archaeological expertise relates to many areas of police work and criminology, including surveying large areas, digging up buried evidence, particularly human remains, and reconstructing facial appearances from the skull (see Hunter et al. 1996). The emerging field of forensic archaeology makes archaeologists not only competent experts but also gives them an immediate social relevance by contributing to the fight against injustice (cf. Cox 2001). The connections between archaeology and criminology do, however, go even further. As cited earlier, Pallottino compared archaeology with a court trial. Michael Shanks describes a similar archaeological court scenario as follows:

> Archaeology is judiciary. The archaeologist is judge and clerk of the court. The past is accused. The finds are witnesses. As in Kafka, we do not really know the charge. There is plenty of mystery. Archaeology follows the process of the law: inquiry (the accused and witnesses are observed and questioned, tortured with spades and trowels); abjudication (the archaeologist reflects on the mystery and gives a verdict); inscription (the archaeologist records trial and sentence, publishes for record of precedence). (1992: 54)

This metaphor was made literal in a staged public inquiry about the meaning of the Cerne Giant in Dorset (Darvill et al. 1999). The giant hill figure was put on trial, as it were, in order to find out what we know about him, how we know what we know, and what it all means. In front of a packed audience, the inquiry took place on March 23, 1996, in the Village Hall at Cerne Abbas. All was filmed by the BBC, who were keen to present the debate as a courtroom drama. Three cases were presented: that the Giant is prehistoric/Romano-British in origin; that he is of medieval or postmedieval origin; and lastly, that he is significant irrespective of age. Tim Darvill, Ronald Hutton, and Barbara Bender acted as advocates for the three arguments. In addition to making their own pleas, they each invited several expert witnesses to strengthen their cases. A panel of assessors steered the inquiry and coordinated cross-examination and third-party questioning of the witnesses. The audience functioned as the jury and finally voted, with a large majority favoring the case for a prehistoric/Romano-British origin.

The Paradigm of Clues

In an often-cited essay, Carlo Ginzburg (1983) argues for the existence of an epistemological paradigm of clues that has developed since the second half of the nineteenth century across several of the humanities. Its origins, however, go back much farther and lie both in hunters' readings of animal tracks and in early divination, which can be seen as reading clues about the future (Huxley 1880). Ginzburg thus established a connection between various fields that share an occupation with reading tiny clues in order to infer their causes. I have already referred to the way modern criminologists and literary detectives such as Hercule Poirot (or indeed Sherlock Holmes) use clues to bring criminals to justice. Another relevant field is art history. Giovanni Morelli developed a method by which unsigned paintings can be attributed to particular artists on the basis of seemingly insignificant details. He argued that the depiction of details such as earlobes, noses, fingernails, and toes follows learned techniques, which become unconscious and unquestioned routines and are thus far more indicative of a particular artist's hand than more conspicuous characteristics that could have been deliberately copied. John Beazley later applied the same idea to the identification of the painters of red- and black-figured Greek pottery. His approach has been very influential in classical archaeology and still has followers today (see Shanks 1996: 37–41; Whitley 1997).

Physicians infer in a similar way from certain symptoms to the cause of a particular disease or pain, and Ginzburg has argued that the paradigm of clues in fact reflects a medical way of thinking. Indeed, both Morelli and Arthur Conan Doyle had been educated as physicians. The same is true for Sigmund Freud, who, in addition, was not only a fan of Sherlock Holmes but also knew some of Morelli's writings (Zintzen 1998: 239). Freud writes on one occasion that in psychoanalysis, as "if you were a detective engaged in tracing a murder," one should never "under-estimate small indications; by their help we may succeed in getting on the track of something bigger" (1961: 27). Freud, too, saw a direct analogy between the methods of Holmes, Morelli, and psychoanalysis, but unlike Ginzburg he also saw the relevance of archaeology in this context. Freud followed with great interest the excavations of his time in Pompeii and Rome in Italy, in Knossos on Crete, and in Troy in Turkey; he visited archaeological museums and was himself a collector of antiquities (see Bernfeld 1951; Ucko 2001). It is therefore not surprising that in his psychoanalytic work Freud compared early childhood with human prehistory, the remains and ruins of which are slowly suppressed and buried as time goes by. Just like an archaeologist recovers fragments of ancient civilizations through excavation, Freud considered the psychoanalyst to be able to locate and reveal, beneath layers of amnesia, the fragmentary memories and remains of the earliest childhood of a patient. Dreams and neurotic personality disorders were his favorite excavation sites (Kuspit 1989; Gere 2002; Thomas 2004: 161–70). Based on the fragments found, however tiny, the psychoanalyst can reconstruct entire emotional constellations. Famously, Freud writes in *Constructions in Analysis* that the occupation of the psychoanalyst resembles, to a great extent, that of the archaeologist:

> The two processes are in fact identical, except that the analyst works under better conditions and has more material at his command to assist him, since what he is dealing with is not something destroyed but something that is still alive. . . . But just as the archaeologist builds up the walls of the building from the foundations that have remained standing, determines the number and position of the columns from depressions in the floor and reconstructs the mural decorations and paintings from the remains found in the débris, so does the analyst proceed when he draws his inferences from the fragments of memories, from the associations and from the behavior of the subject of the analysis. (p. 259)

Although Ginzburg did not refer to archaeology, it is clear that the discipline of archaeology has not only been influenced by the idea of inferring causes from clues but has shaped this paradigm too (cf. Zintzen 1998; Gere 2002). The example of Sigmund Freud shows that the paradigm of clues, which Ginzburg derives from medicine, can also be firmly linked to archaeology. It is worth noting in this context that even the archcriminological method of using fingerprints as decisive clues for identifying culprits unambiguously has as one of its origins the study of finger marks on prehistoric pots (Beavan 2002: 69).

Spurensicherung Art

In 1974 an exhibition in the German cities of Hamburg and Munich, titled "Spurensicherung," brought a group of previously unconnected artists together. *Spurensicherung* is the process of "securing circumstantial evidence" and (as a noun) also is the German term used for the forensics department of the Police, which locates and records material clues found at crime scenes. In this case the term referred to a number of artists who shared an interest in material leftovers and recording techniques. Among them were Christian Boltanski, Paul-Armand Gette, Nikolaus Lang, Patrick and Anne Poirier, and Charles Simonds. Recently, others such as Mark Dion, Susan Hiller, and Nigel Poor (figure 4.1) have followed a similar direction in their work, and they too can be associated with the *Spurensicherung* theme (see Metken 1977; 1996; Schneider 1985; A. Schneider 1993; Putnam 2001).

For an archaeologist there are different possible reactions to artworks such as these. On the one hand, one might say that art is art and archaeology is archaeology. Neither Anne or Patrick Poirier nor Mark Dion nor, in fact, any of the other artists associated with the *Spurensicherung* art claims to be an archaeologist in the sense of wanting to advance our knowledge of what actually happened in the past. Despite the care and exactness displayed, this is not scientific practice, and no hypotheses or interpretations about any events in the past are actually being offered. The way they copy, or parody, scientific and especially archaeological methods would then have no bearing on the academic discipline of archaeology at all. There are, however, other ways of interpreting these works.

The works of the *Spurensicherung* can be taken as a criticism of archaeology as a scientific discipline: by seemingly adopting its forms but denouncing its content, *Spurensicherung* art is a plea against the "scien-

DECEMBER

Figure 4.1 Nigel Poor's *Month of December* from her art project Found (1998). She writes (abbreviated from web.archive.org/web/20020302060905/http://www .hainesgallery.com/NP.statement.html): "On January 1, 1998, I began a project called **FOUND**. It is a journal of time, the environment, and of myself. Everyday I took a walk to collect something outside—in streets and alleys, playgrounds and fields, gutters and lawns. The objects were clues to hidden worlds. It is as if each object had fallen from a story, and, in its finding, was plucked out of the obscurity of some invisible narrative. In this sense, the object became 'evidence' which deserved closer inspection. These lost objects—these dumb things—present a concrete if oblique account of a year's day-by-day appearance, and disappearance, and in doing so catalyze a remembrance of one's own passing of time." Every print of her photographs has been branded by a letter-press stating the date and exact location of where the depicted object was found. Reproduced by permission.

Mark Dion

Mark Dion is an American artist who has been inspired by scientific practices in the natural sciences and, more recently, by archaeology. In some of his earlier works, Dion makes references to naturalists of the eighteenth and nineteenth centuries, who investigated natural history by exploring, collecting, and classifying exotic specimens in remote parts of the world. In particular, he parodied their working practices, both in the field and in the laboratory, as well as their resulting publications and the associated cabinets of curiosities they exhibited. One such work is entitled "The Taxonomy of Non-Endangered Species" (1990) and shows Mickey Mouse on a ladder in front of a shelf with labeled jars containing toy animals in alcohol. In another project, "A Meter of Jungle" (1992), Dion removed a cubic meter of soil from the Brazilian rainforest, moved it into the exhibition room, where he sorted and classified its content, and finally displayed his collection.

A quasiarchaeological site of the future was created in the form of a complete contemporary children's room with a multitude of objects showing dinosaur images, entitled "When Dinosaurs Ruled the Earth (Toys R U.S.)" (1994). But Dion's most archaeological works were his various "digs" for artifacts. One project, the "Tate Thames Dig" of 1999/2000, involved Dion and his team of volunteer field workers extensively beachcombing along the foreshore of the Thames River in London in the United Kingdom (figure 4.2). The objects found were then cleaned, identified, and classified, all taking place as a public performance outside London's Tate Gallery. Finally, all finds (including bones, toys, broken glass, and credit cards) were systematically ordered and displayed in a large curiosity cabinet and five treasure chests inside the Tate Gallery. Dion once stated programmatically, "During my digs into trash dumps of previous centuries I'm not interested in one moment or type of object, but each artifact—be it yesterday's Juicy Fruit wrapper or a sixteenth-century porcelain fragment—is treated the same" (cited in Corrin et al. 1997: 30).

Sources: Dion 1997; Corrin et al. 1997; Coles and Dion 1999

Figure 4.2 Mark Dion and collaborators at the Tate Thames Dig, 1999. Photograph © 1999 by Andrew Cross, reproduced by permission.

tification" of our world (Borbein 1981: 50). Works of the *Spurensicherung* often express very personal associations, desires, or memories that have been buried and would be irretrievable by the application of the scientific meticulousness and diligence that is caricatured. But there are treasures to be discovered beyond "objective" knowledge, calling for alternative methods of recovery. To a certain extent, their value lies precisely in the fact that archaeology or any other science cannot lift them. In this sense, *Spurensicherung* art is something like antiarchaeology. It questions the authority of the archaeologists by pointing to the nonscientific, i.e., all those aspects of life that scientists may miss but that are even more elementary and significant. In this sense, these artworks constitute a powerful critique of archaeology and related disciplines voiced not through discursive writing but through material practice (Schneider 1993: 3).

Although the artists concerned may not always have intended it, the works of the *Spurensicherung* also demonstrate why the paradigm of clues is an illusion that depends on questionable premises and is ultimately of less use to archaeology or any of the other sciences mentioned than commonly assumed. *Spurensicherung* art portrays archaeology as discovery, documentation, recovery, classification, and description of material remains that are ultimately taken to reveal in themselves certain truths about the past. The act of securing and reading of material evidence as clues appeals to people precisely because of the immediacy of the physical artifacts involved (figure 4.3). Material clues seem to connect a contemporary audience directly with the particular individual who once left them behind. As Mark Dion explains in a January 6, 2002, newspaper article in *The New York Times* regarding a new "digging" project of his, "A fragment of blue-and-white willow export porcelain thrown away in 1894 lies inert for 107 years until someone from the dig team finds it, creating a momentary bridge to the person who lost or threw the object away." This not only creates a sense of aura and authenticity (as discussed in chapter 7) but also an admiration for the archaeologist who can make such things "speak" and bring the past back to life. It is, however, a mistake to believe that an archaeologist, or for that matter a criminologist, can immediately reconstruct the past from simply collecting, recording, and classifying some material remains and traces that function as clues. What are really only the first few steps of the interpretive process, the *Spurensicherung* art seemingly takes as its ultimate aim, thus failing to appreciate what archaeologists actually do (as argued by Schneider 1985, 1999; Flaig 1999). This is plain for all to see in that the final outcome of *Spurensicherung* works are generally collections of artifacts rather than any specific claims about the past, and that becomes very clear, for example, in the archaeological models and documentations produced by the artists Anne and Patrick Poirier (see sidebar below). Insofar as archaeological assemblages of artifacts remain mere collections of material evidence, they, too, fail in becoming meaningful in relation to what happened in the past.

The *Spurensicherung* ignores the fact that after an archaeological find or feature has been perceived and classified as such, both already acts of interpretation (see Holtorf 2002), it needs to be assessed further as to its meaning and significance in the given archaeological context. All of these are interpretive processes that depend on the approaches, methodologies, and research interests of the archaeologists in the present. This is a central insight of a recently developed approach known as "interpretive archaeology" (e.g., Tilley 1993; Thomas 1996: 62–63). The British archaeologist

Figure 4.3 Nostalgia for the present in David Macaulay's drawing *Gas Station* (1978). Plate from *Great Moments in Architecture*, © 1978 by David Macaulay. Reprinted by permission of Houghton Mifflin Company.

Anne and Patrick Poirier

Anne and Patrick Poirier were both born in 1942, and their later art was strongly influenced by their having grown up in France after the devastations of World War II. The experience visiting in 1970 the ruins of Buddhist temples in Angkor in Cambodia led them to become interested in the concept and idea of archaeology. Since then Anne and Patrick Poirier have been calling themselves archaeologists, and their work has circled around two related issues: the fragility and destruction of cultures and civilizations, and the importance of collective memory. As Anne Poirier put it once in a discussion in 1998: "Our work is about the possibility of the past and the impossibility of the future."

A good example of their work is *Ostia Antica* (1971–1972), based on an extended visit of the archaeological site that was the harbor of ancient Rome. This work consisted of several parts: first, a large (three-meter-long) plan of ancient Ostia, based on their own explorations, that resembles (but is not identical to) an archaeological site plan; second, a large miniature model of the ruined town (eleven by six meters) based on the plan and their own memories; third, a series of impressions of house parts and walls; and finally, several notebooks containing descriptions of their experiences, as well as a few pressed flowers and some soil. It is immediately obvious that the piece does not attempt to reconstruct the ancient site but rather serves as a kind of rebirth of the ruined town in the present. The aim is not to record objectively an archaeological site or to teach us anything about ancient Ostia, but to document meticulously a very personal experience of the remains of this site and thereby to provide a commentary about issues such as aging, decay, and remembrance.

Similar ideas were evoked in several, more recently completed, large works by the Poiriers, which were devoted to Mnemosyne, the ancient goddess of memory and mother of the nine muses. Influenced by Mnemosyne's significance to Aby Warburg, these works make reference to the idea of a library and express an architectural understanding of memory in the brain. On the occasion of the opening of one of the *Mnemosyne* exhibitions, a card invited guests to "the presentation of the latest archeological finds made during the excavation 1990–1991 on the site of 'Mnemosyne.'" This presentation was said to draw on the enormous collection by an anonymous architect/archaeologist of documents, photographs, fragments and remains, plans, notes, and models from the site of Mnemosyne. One set of exhibits was called 'The Archive of the Archaeologist' and consisted of chests of drawers containing things like an image, a fragment, an illustrated journal, and a little model of a brain cut in half to show the remains of an ancient temple inside (see figure 4.4).

Sources: Metken 1977: 57–76; Poirier and Poirier 1994; Jussen 1999

John Barrett (1994: 71) put its core idea very succinctly: "Our knowledge is not grounded upon the material evidence itself, but arises from the interpretive strategies which we are prepared to bring to bear upon that evidence."

The same could be said not only for hunters following tracks and detectives following clues but also for physicians acting on the basis of symptoms, psychoanalysts making much of remembered details, and art historians inferring from tiny divergences. In each case interpretation first creates the clues and then makes them significant in a particular way. In this sense the difference between traces and messages is much smaller than sometimes assumed. It is, for example, not always clear what is a trace, what is a message, and what is both. They each require equal amounts of interpretation to become meaningful. In the end all the hunter, the detective, the physician, the psychoanalyst, the art historian, and the archaeologist can offer are plausible interpretations that may or may not persuade others (cf. Veit et al. 2003).

In as much as the works of the *Spurensicherung* and the paradigm of clues generally imply a clear and undisputable relation between causes in the past and visible (recordable, collectable) effects in the present, they are misleading. Every clue can always be read in different ways, pointing to different causes. Thus, nothing may be more difficult to predict than the past, and the paradigm of clues is ultimately far less significant for understanding the past than often assumed. What are significant, however, are particular contexts and discourses of interpretation (as discussed in the following chapters).

Archaeology as Process and Desire

Arguably, artists of the *Spurensicherung* tradition in any case do not wish to represent how archaeologists understand the past from its material remains. What appears to matter far more to them than arriving at a particular reconstruction are the first parts of that journey, which are characterized by a particular kind of thinking and experience. In this sense, the main reference point of the *Spurensicherung* is not the past but the symbolic act of remembering (Himmelmann 1976: 174). The works presented are modern constructions that cite archaeological method but ultimately make statements about their own present. As the art critic Günter Metken (1977: 14) puts it, the *Spurensicherung* is not the search for an original condition, but the ruins, remains, and traces provide an opportunity to define the artist's own position in the present. As in the archaeological adventure of hunting for treasure (see chapter 3), it is not the final result that counts but the process the artist goes through to get there (Renfrew 2003: 103–6).

At the beginning of this chapter I cited Pallottino's words about the similarities between archaeological research and criminal investigation. Significantly, he continues by speculating about whether it is the process of hunting for and interpreting clues that makes archaeology "so exciting to the general public, who derive such enjoyment from reading detective stories or following the twists and turns of court cases." Could it therefore

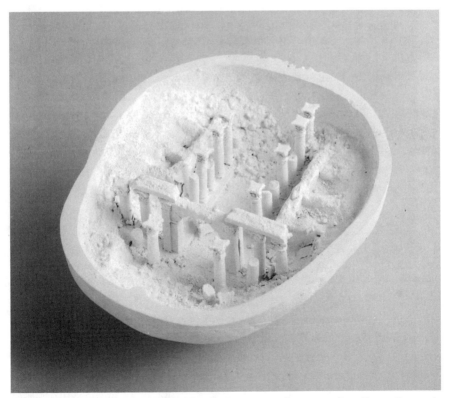

Figure 4.4 Anne and Patrick Poirier, Petit paysage dans un crâne. From the work *Mnémosyne, Les archives de l'archéologue,* 1991. **Source: Poirier and Poirier 1994, 160. Reproduced by permission.**

be that archaeology too makes a particular journey rather than seeks to arrive at a particular destination, that archaeology too is a symbolic act of remembering, which provides an opportunity for us all to define our own position in the present? Is archaeology only in a technical sense concerned with the past but otherwise concerned with present and future as the classical archaeologist Adolf Borbein (1981: 57–58) contemplated already more than twenty years ago? More recently, Barrett has expressed a related idea:

> There is no actual past state of history "out there" which is represented by our data and which is waiting for us to discover it. . . . All we have are the contexts of our desires to know a past, positions from which we may then examine the material conditions which others, at other times and from other perspectives, also sought to understand. We should treat this material as a medium from which it is always possible to create meaning, rather than a record which is involved in the transmission of meaning. (1994: 169–70)

Besides the creation of meaning on an excavation, archaeology as a present process has many other facets too. It springs from a will to know the past but can also involve the desire to collect antiquities or to save ancient sites from destruction, among other things (see Shanks 1992 for more!). As Gavin Lucas (1997: 9) states, to complete these processes would frustrate the very desires that lie behind it. The British archaeologist and author Paul Bahn confirmed this when he argued in an interview that it would be "a great pity" if we ever managed to understand all the secrets of the past (www.oxbowbooks.com/feature.cfm/FeatureID/76/Location/Oxbow, accessed October 4, 2004).

Thesis 6:
The process of doing archaeology is more important than its results.

Archaeology is not a question of needs being eventually fulfilled but of deeply felt desires being sustained. These desires can have erotic overtones (see chapter 2). The search for the past is at the same time the search for ourselves. As a consequence, we never quite know enough about the past, a collection of antiquities is never really complete, there are never nearly sufficient numbers of sites being saved, and often there does not even seem to be sufficient time for syntheses of what has been achieved already or at times for any publication at all. The archaeological process must therefore go on continuously.

Incidentally, the same might be said for the processes of historical, criminological, and medical research, as well as for psychoanalytic treatment. Their benefit lies, at least partly, in seeing them continue, and not necessarily in any specific outcome. From a similar perspective, the American psychiatrist Donald Spence (1987) has proposed an alternative to Freud's "archaeological" way of defining psychoanalysis by suggesting that it is actually more like a constant rereading of the same situation. This alternative might even have some relevance for archaeology itself:

> In arguing for an accumulation of commentaries rather than the excavation of a session (or a person's mind), we are saying goodbye to the archaeological metaphor and substituting something much closer to an open conversation. We are suggesting that wisdom does not emerge by searching for historical truth, continually frustrated . . . by a lack of clear specimens and [biased] data; rather, wisdom emerges from the gradual accumulation of different readings of the same situation and the accumulating overlay of new contexts. Notice how the metaphor has changed. No meaning attaches to any one piece that is buried in the past, in the unconscious, or in the clinician's incomplete records; no excavation is necessary. Instead, the meanings are constantly in flux, seen each time against a different context which provides a change of emphasis. (Spence 1987: 179–80)

Archaeology, too, can be taken to provide a collection of ever changing creative commentaries about the past and its remains. Each of these does not offer a contribution to an eventually complete reconstruction of the past, but they reflect the constantly changing approaches of those commentating. Arguably, this is precisely what the paradigm of clues has in practice always been used for. It may not have to offer any special opportunities to reconstruct the past, but it provides frameworks for following animals, convicting criminals, exciting readers, healing patients, and comparing paintings. In none of these cases does it ultimately matter whether (from the perspective of an omniscient observer) a certain trace has been understood correctly or not, as the reference to the trace as a clue for something else is already meaningful and suggestive in itself (figure 4.5).

It is precisely this engagement with material clues and associated commentaries about the past that accounts for much of the popular fasci-

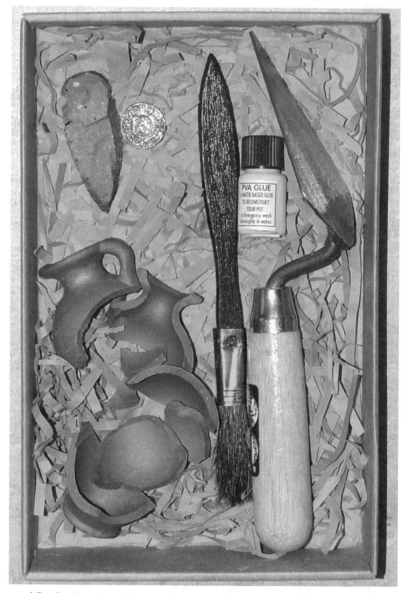

Figure 4.5 Archaeology Kit on sale at UK heritage sites. This "Gift for Pleasure" from the company Flights of Fancy (www.flightsoffancy.co.uk) provides children with a fairly wide-ranging booklet about archaeology but mostly with the paraphernalia of archaeological practice: a trowel, a brush, some replica artifacts and a broken little vase that can be reassembled using the glue supplied. This pack is not about adventurous fieldwork or making great discoveries, but about exercising archaeological practices such as trowelling on the surface, brushing a find, reassembling a vase, and studying artifacts as material clues. Photograph by Cornelius Holtorf, 2002.

nation with archaeology. This may be one reason why the British TV documentary series *Time Team*, which has recently broadcast its tenth series, has been extremely successful for so long. Its normal format is a one-hour program documenting a three-day archaeological excavation at a chosen site. The highlights of each program are the moments when the presenter, Tony Robinson, gets called over to look at a newly discovered material clue and the subsequent discussion, which is often followed up by expert analysis about its significance in relation to what happened at the site in the past. The latest *Time Team* book (Robinson and Aston 2002) takes a similar approach, and its press release proclaims that "archaeology has never been so much fun. This book will inspire everyone to get out into their back gardens and start digging." Archaeological programs on the Discovery Channel often follow this format, too. Another great example is the *Amelia Earhart Project*, a team of volunteers, both amateurs and professionals, including archaeologists, that devotes much of its time to the hunt for the remains of Earhart's plane lost in 1937 in the Pacific, seemingly without a trace. The extensive account of their research so far is compelling, not because the mystery may (or may not) be solved but to a large extent because of the engagement with the materiality of the disappeared plane and its crew and with the kinds of clues that could be left of it and where (King et al. 2001; see also www.tighar.org/Projects/Earhart/AEoverview.html). In the end, therefore, archaeology and *Spurensicherung* art can find a common denominator after all. They do not share all the same practices nor, indeed, their main aims, but both offer commentaries about material remains of the past in the present. It could therefore be said that *Spurensicherung* is as much a kind of archaeology as archaeology is a kind of *Spurensicherung*.

All of this should not be taken to imply that there have been (or indeed are) no other ways of interpreting ancient sites or artifacts than either as clues as to past human actions or as media to express various concerns of the present. The next two chapters therefore take a look at how dramatically the meanings of ancient sites and artifacts have changed over time and at the wide range of interpretations and meanings that can be found regarding them in various contexts of the present.

CHAPTER FIVE
PAST MEANINGS

Every age has the Stonehenge it deserves—or desires.

—Jacquetta Hawkes (1967: 174)

I f, as I argue in the previous chapter, all interpretation depends on context and contexts vary, it becomes imperative to study this variety of meanings and interpretations of any object we want to understand. First, in this chapter I discuss the dramatic changes of meanings of archaeological sites and artifacts over time, whereas in the next chapter I emphasize the variety of meanings observed in our own present. I will argue that the variety of these meanings can be truly enormous, even if one and the same site or artifact may be concerned. Indeed, contrary to common assumptions, there is no clear way to separate the "real" meaning of a site or artifact (its "essence") from any "secondary" or "wrong" meanings. How archaeologists and others view and make sense of an object is no more or less appropriate for that object than what others may have thought in the past or may think now.

Life Histories of Things

One way to study archaeological sites and artifacts is to look at them as if they have "life histories" (for further discussion of this metaphor, see Holtorf 2002). Like human bodies, things that have once been born appear to live as what they are until they die. They may have been used and interpreted in different ways along the way, but their material identity appears to remain unchangeable and to have been continuous all along: a megalith seemingly consisted of the same assemblage of stones and earth, among other things, whether it was preserved as a (pre-)historic site, used as a quarry, or painted by a Romanticist painter. Things can reach very different ages, from a few moments to many millennia, but once dead only a few are brought back to life as antiquities or recycled items, effectively

78

enjoying new meanings in new lives. All other things are discarded some-where and often left to disintegrate by themselves.

Accounts of things' life histories are their biographies. In an often-cited passage of an influential article, Igor Kopytoff proposes some general guidelines on how to write the biography of a thing:

> In doing the biography of a thing, one would ask questions similar to those one asks about people: What, sociologically, are the biographical possibilities inherent in its "status" and in the period and culture, and how are these possibilities realized? Where does the thing come from and who made it? What had been its career so far, and what do people consider to be an ideal career for such things? What are the recognized "ages" or periods in the thing's "life," and what are the cultural markers for them? How does the thing's use change with its age, and what happens to it when it reaches the end of its usefulness? (1986: 66–67)

Michael Schiffer (e.g., Schiffer with Miller 1999) and others have studied such life histories of things in order to *infer* from them the observable patterns of their subsequent deposition in the soil. In order to understand the archaeological record of past life, it is essential for them to know how in that past things have been going through sequences of production, use, and eventual discard. Archaeologists like Christopher Tilley (1996: chapter 6), Julian Thomas (1996: chapter 6) and Andy Jones (2002: chapters 5–7), however, have been interested in the life histories of things in a different way. They have published detailed case studies about Neolithic artifacts in which they wanted to *learn* from their various depositional contexts about the meanings and social roles of things in the past. They started from the insight that persons can form parts of things, and things form parts of persons. Andy Jones, for example, argued that the production and use of a specific kind of Neolithic pottery vessel (Grooved ware) was closely allied to the expression of certain forms of social identity. In particular, the consumption of food within these containers was linked with competitive feasting during which important social relations were expressed and confirmed (Jones 2002: chapter 7). Archaeologists can thus use material evidence to study how things once helped to define and redefine relationships between people.

Interestingly, many life-history studies, including those I referred to above, share the assumption that the life of a thing starts at the time of its manufacture and ends at the time of its deposition in the ground. Discarded things are, of course, subjected to all sorts of natural processes, but their lives are commonly deemed over: they become rubbish, ruins, mummies. However, from an alternative perspective, the life histories of things do not end with deposition but continue until the present day: activities such as discovery, recovery, analysis, interpretation, archiving, and exhibiting are processes in the lives of things, too. The meanings of things are constantly changing, even today. They cannot be reduced to a single meaning or significance in the past. Such long life histories can relate not only to prehistoric monuments and entire landscapes, but they can also follow the changing fortunes of various kinds of artifacts. Effectively, they trace the history of cultural memories and *Geschichtskulturen* (see Holtorf 2000–2004 and chapter 1).

Thesis 7:
The meanings of archaeological sites and artifacts have always been changing and cannot be fixed.

In the following I discuss two case studies of such long life histories, one for stone axes and the other for monuments, both first made or constructed during the Neolithic (i.e., roughly five millennia ago). In one case, the object is portable and can physically move between contexts. In the other case, all relevant meanings are brought to a single place and are thus site specific. To make the point clearly, I will focus mostly on various processes after the end of the Neolithic. As will become clear, the chosen examples have particularly rich and interesting life histories, but the general concept of sites and artifacts having lives equally applies to examples that lack any significant amount of human attention, sometimes over very long periods.

Neolithic Stone Axes

Stone axes had rich meanings in prehistory. Recent research in Ireland, the United Kingdom, and Scandinavia led to a better understanding of the special character of Neolithic quarries and production sites, the contemporary long-distance exchange of exotic axes, and their frequent deposition in sacred places such as graves and bogs (Cooney 2000: 188–211; Tilley 1996: chapter 6). All this points to the important roles of stone axes in ritual activities during the Neolithic.

The subsequent lives of prehistoric stone axes and other artifacts have previously been studied in the context of archaeological source criticism. For example, in Mecklenburg-Vorpommern Neolithic axes (or substantial fragments of them) were found in various burial and settlement contexts of the Bronze and Iron ages (see Holtorf 2000–2004: 5.1.4). In Sweden, a stone axe was found with a runic inscription possibly reminding us, "Oltha owns this axe." This must have been engraved in or around the time of the Vikings. In addition, both ends were damaged, possibly due to pounding in order to gain a powerful medicine (Blinkenberg 1911: 91). Such cases were noted as a warning to archaeologists that modern records of stone axes may reflect not their Neolithic patterns of use and discard but later activities that effectively disturbed the earlier record and, thus, might confuse our interpretations (e.g., Reitinger 1976: 536).

It is perhaps more interesting to study what these finds actually meant to post-Neolithic communities. The stone axes had probably been found and picked up on ploughed fields, much as they are today. It is well known that Neolithic stone axes have, in various classical, medieval, and modern contexts mostly in Europe and Asia, been interpreted as thunderbolts that originated from the sky and contained magical powers. This theory was supported by the fact that they were often found in the fields after heavy rainfalls. People collected and used them as amulets and lucky charms, healing remedies, or for the protection of buildings against lightning (see figure 5.1; Blinkenberg 1911; Barner 1957; Reitinger 1976; Carelli 1997). Such meanings could also account for at least some of the reuses of stone axes during later prehistoric and early historic periods. In the seventeenth century Samuel Butler's poem *Hudibras* (2002 [1663]) very clearly mentions axes with a drilled hole (Part II, Canto III, 291–92):

Chace evil spirits away by dint
Of cickle, horse-shoe, hollow-flint;

As recently as at the beginning of the Franco-Prussian War in 1870, conscripted soldiers rushed into pharmacies (!) to buy thunderbolts to protect them against bullets (Reitinger 1976: 534). Only a few years ago, in 1988 two stone axes could be seen near the apex of the roof of a farm building in Rothemühl, Kreis Ueckermünde, Germany. Other axes have been used during the twentieth century as a candlestick, a loom weight, and a clock

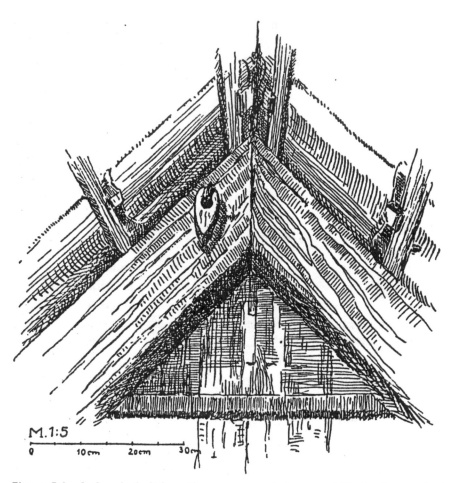

Figure 5.1   A thunderbolt in action or a reused stone-axe? Protection against lightning on the roof of a German barn. Source: W. Barner. 1957. Von Kultäxten, Beilzauber und rituellem Bohren. *Die Kunde* N. F. 8: 175–86, figure 2.

weight (Reitinger 1976: 518). Evidence such as this provides much more than a cautionary note for using distribution maps in order to study the Neolithic. It provides us with an entry point into the eventful lives of these artifacts themselves. In effect, it is not at all a simple question to ask to which period a given stone axe belongs. The best answer may be that it belongs to several.

Significantly, the later uses of stone axes do not necessarily represent a survival in folk memory from much earlier ritual uses of similar objects.

Instead, found stone axes may have been more or less spontaneously appreciated for their physical and associative social or metaphysical qualities. Individual life histories of prehistoric objects show a wide range of particular motives as to why prehistoric finds can be given significance and meaning in later ages and up to the present day. The circumstances of how dominant interpretations of particular classes of artifacts first emerge and then change over time are worth studying in their own right. One good example is the transformation of thunderbolts into stone axes during the second half of the seventeenth century, to which the Swedish archaeologist Ola Jensen (1999) has devoted some attention.

Since the establishment of the discipline of archaeology, the stone axes have been widely seen as archaeological evidence from prehistoric periods: they have become clues to understanding the past. Some are now museum exhibits in prehistoric collections, others may be for sale at auctions. But these contexts too are just episodes in their lives. They only happen to be the contexts within which some of us encounter these objects. My own present context is the sole reason why I speak of stone axes that were once interpreted as thunderbolts and used in ritual, and not of thunderbolts that are currently considered to have been made by ancient people and are displayed in glass cases. Arguably, the only common denominator among these constantly changing meanings and significances of archaeological artifacts is that none would have been shared by the people who first made them (Ucko 2001: 307).

Prehistoric Monuments

As far as monuments are concerned, the situation is similar to that of stone axes: both had long lives and, in many cases, remain alive today. Intriguingly, the British prehistorian Richard Bradley has pointed out that continuous reinterpretations are part of the "very logic of monument building" (1993). Many monuments of all times were designed to outlive their builders. But whether the intentions of the monument builders were fulfilled in later ages or not, the continuing histories show clearly that many megaliths succeeded in their own terms. Monuments built during the Neolithic had long and exciting histories for centuries and millennia, and some are still very much part of current affairs even in our own age (see Daniel 1972; Holtorf 2000–2004).

CHAPTER 5

The Changing Meanings of Stonehenge

The late British archaeologist Jacquetta Hawkes once famously declared that every age has the Stonehenge it deserves—or desires (1967: 174). The long life history of this famous British site certainly bears this out, and it is not surprising that this monument has attracted many biographers, including Christopher Chippindale (1994) and Barbara Bender (1998). They all demonstrate that Stonehenge has been an obstacle and a mysterious ruin in the landscape for longer than it ever was a prehistoric ritual site.

Occupation of the area begins in the Mesolithic, but Stonehenge itself and many of the surrounding ritual sites were built in the Neolithic between circa 3100 and 2300 BC. During the Bronze Age the stones were rearranged several times, a dagger was famously carved into one of them, and many barrows were erected along the horizon around the site. From the late Bronze Age (circa 1600 BC) onwards, the picture changed completely as Stonehenge seems to have lost its ritual meaning and agricultural field systems came to dominate the entire area.

Julie Gardiner (Cleal et al. 1995: 332) describes the subsequent story of Stonehenge as "essentially one of dilapidation, vandalism, occasional use, and restoration, its main role being as a tourist attraction." Evidence for occasional visits has been found from the Iron Age and the Roman, post-Roman, medieval, and postmedieval periods. There is no reason to suppose that people of these times viewed Stonehenge with any less interest and curiosity than we do today, but this did not stop others from acts of vandalism and stone robbery.

The first known descriptions of the monument are those of Henry of

In previous research I investigated the changing fate of approximately twelve hundred megaliths in the northern German region of Mecklenburg-Vorpommern (Holtorf 2000–2004). As this in-depth case study demonstrates the dramatic changes that can take place in the lives of a single set of archaeological objects, I will summarize the main results. The impressive megalithic tombs of the area were built within a relatively short period during the middle Neolithic (Schuldt 1972). After their construction many megaliths were used for several centuries for various types of burials. By the early Bronze Age, all the ancient graves had ceased to be used as burial places and were formally closed by filling the chambers with earth. The formal closing of the megaliths ends in all cases a more or less continuous tradition of understanding these monuments as burial sites.

Huntington and Geoffrey of Monmouth, both writing in the twelfth century. From the sixteenth century onwards, documented interest increased steadily. Regular fairs were held there, and antiquarians like John Aubrey and William Stukeley marveled at the stones. Stonehenge became one of the first tourist sites in Europe, and already in 1822 a guardian took up residence near the stones to protect them from damage and discourage littering. In 1901 the site was fenced in, and an entrance fee was introduced. Scheduled in 1913, the transfer of Stonehenge into state property was accomplished in 1918. Major archaeological excavations and restoration work were carried out during the 1950s and 1960s. The 1970s saw the fencing in of the stones themselves due to erosion resulting from vast numbers of visitors. Although celebrations at midsummer sunrise had started long before, the same decade also saw the beginning of the annual Stonehenge Free Festival. After the 1985 Battle of the Beanfield between some festivalers and the police, the former were kept out of Stonehenge by major annual security operations of the latter. Free access at summer solstice was finally reintroduced in 1999, so far without further confrontation. Far from being a tranquil antiquity, Stonehenge may have been more politically disputed during the end of the twentieth century than at any time beforehand. Stonehenge has also consistently been one of the most popular tourist destinations in the United Kingdom, with over eight hundred thousand visitors in 1999. At the same time, various druid orders and new pagans consider Stonehenge today as one of their most sacred sites.

Sources: Chippindale 1994; Cleal et al. 1995; Cresswell 1996: chapter 4; Bender 1998.

Many megaliths were preserved as they were or adapted to new uses but not destroyed. Finds of all periods from the later Bronze Age to the medieval period have been made in up to a third of the excavated megalithic mounds (in some areas), both within the mounds as well as within the chambers themselves. They can hardly all be explained by accidental deposits during work carried out in modern times by antiquarians, treasure hunters, or stone robbers, especially since more than half of these finds were, in the eyes of the excavators, obviously or possibly connected with later burials (see below). These finds therefore seem to indicate human presence and activity during later periods at a fairly large number of megaliths, probably indicating that these sites held some special meaning. Curiosity about the strange mounds containing huge stones and

Figure 5.2   This German car ad (1994) for the Pontiac Trans Sport carried the slogan, "More Science than Fiction," and went on to explain that it is "no miracle if you feel magically attracted to the Trans Sport. After all, its futuristic aura inspires all the senses. A true work of art behind which the most modern technology is hidden putting time and space at the individual's disposal"(my translation). Image courtesy of McCann-Erickson, Deutschland, reproduced by permission.

sometimes human bones could have motivated people, perhaps especially children, to spend afternoons there, exploring further. Such investigations might well have been the earliest form of archaeological research (cf. Hingley 1996: 242). The possible insight that these sites were in fact old graves may have paved the way for subsequent burials in the same mounds.

Burials of later ages occurred on average in one of every six excavated megaliths, which together contain evidence of up to eighty buried individuals. On the island of Rügen the proportion was twice as large. To give one example, in Dummertevitz on Rügen at least nine, and perhaps as many as twenty, Slavic urns were buried at a megalith, which at that time appears to have been completely covered by a mound. Nevertheless, the urns were carefully placed in relation to key architectural features, right on top of the original grave chamber, indicating that the mourners were aware of the overall layout and content of the Neolithic burial chamber. Although people were perhaps understandably glad sometimes to find a mound already built in which they could bury their dead, it is likely that it was also important to them that these mounds constituted ancient burial sites. In another context Bradley (1993: chapter 6) interprets deliberate architectural references to past monuments as legitimation attempts by political elites concerned with inventing a "fictitious genealogy" and thus establishing an imagined long-term continuity of their power. Burials in ancient barrows may have been a convenient method for inventing ancestral genealogies on which claims for political power could be based. But certain nostalgic feelings, the expression of a particular social identity or of social prestige, or special cosmological significance attributed to these sites could explain equally well the choice of ancient mounds for later burials.

When new graves or monuments were built during later ages, they did not fill empty and untouched spaces but were fitted into a landscape of ancient sites that were meaningful. Thus, later monuments often relate to earlier monuments, taking them as reference points for messages about continuity or the change of social identity. Circular or rectangular stone settings surrounding burials, for example, were not only features of megalithic mounds (Schuldt 1972: 63–69), but occurred also in the Bronze Age, the pre-Roman Iron Age, and the Slavic period. Whether this tradition was continuous or invented is less important than the likelihood that a reference to known ancient monuments was intended—or at least also observed at the time itself. It may have been important for people's social identities to display inspirations from the past and show commitment to traditional values in the architecture of their graves (see Hingley 1996: 240–41). Stone settings surrounding prehistoric burial mounds could also have self-evidently signified the border between the world of the living and that of the dead, and they might therefore have been built in similar ways at different times.

Likewise, the frequent similarity in diameter and height of barrows from earlier and later periods may indicate that ancient architecture was consciously imitated in later ages. It is conceivable that mounds erected during the Bronze Age, the pre-Roman Iron Age, or the Slavic period gained some of their cultural meanings from their obvious similarity to the earlier Neolithic mounds that were sometimes located directly next to them. Because of the similarity between megalithic mounds and Bronze Age barrows, both have often been mixed up in the terminology of early antiquarians, and even modern excavations have discovered megaliths when they expected Bronze Age burials (see Holtorf 2000–2004: 5.1.6). In several cases megaliths were even physically converted into tumuli during the Bronze Age. This, too, may reflect deliberate attempts to gain prestige and status by manipulating genealogies or inventing ancient traditions (cf. Hingley 1996: 240–41). Affirming a particular view of the past can also be a powerful method to resist change. The Slavs may have shown considerable interest in prehistoric burial mounds, reusing and imitating them, when they were threatened by an expanding German Empire that tried to force its rule and the Christian religion (and burial customs) onto them. After the successful Christianization of Mecklenburg-Vorpommern, megaliths ceased to have the same appeal to people and were in some cases associated with pagan forebears and indeed the Devil. The lives of megaliths had entered a new phase.

Since the medieval period the material properties of megaliths occasionally led to the destruction of the tombs and the reuse of their stones for purposes such as building houses, roads, and churches. Even during the twentieth century, the capstones of megaliths were in several cases, as in Hamberge, removed from the grave and used for war and other memorials (figure 5.3). It cannot, of course, be ruled out that ancient monuments were valued for their stone material in earlier periods too, whether this led to a partial demolition or to a rededication in situ. At the megalith of Nobbin, it could be shown that a large capstone had already, in the pre-Roman Iron Age, been removed from the grave and possibly reused elsewhere (Holtorf 2000–2004: 8.1). The desecration inherent in such

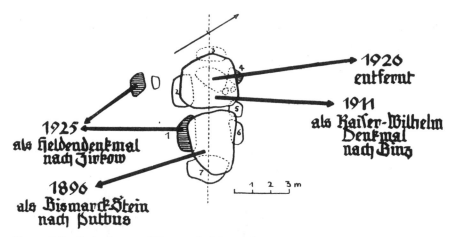

Figure 5.3   A single megalith recycled for various memorials on Rügen, Germany. Source: W. Hansen. 1933. Zur Verbreitung der Riesensteingräber in Norddeutschland. *Mannus* **25: 347.**

actions and vandalism at ancient monuments in general are the consequences of a wanted or accepted change of meaning (see chapter 8). They
can be done out of indifference or quite deliberately in opposition to other
meanings and practices. Just as the past can be manipulated and traditions
invented by the construction of monuments, continuities can also be hidden and pasts denied by the destruction of monuments. In certain circumstances, such as political or religious upheavals, ancient sites have
intentionally been demolished. In others they have become rubbish
dumps, which provides another possible explanation for the later finds
made at and in megaliths.

Postmedieval finds have only very rarely been made in, at, or near
megaliths. But this does not prove that the land around megaliths was
abandoned or that megaliths had lost all meanings. People simply did not
leave many traces there at that time. It can be assumed that megaliths
were then, as some are still today, associated with various folktales. To
judge from collections of the nineteenth century, tales about the Devil and
stories about giants were particularly widespread, a fact reflected in names
of megaliths such as *Teufelsbackofen* ("Devil's oven") and *Riesenbett*
("giant's bed"). The most common term for megaliths in the older literature and in popular culture until the present day is *Hünengrab* ("giant's
grave"), which may reflect the assumptions of a time when the activities
of giants provided the best explanation for these large stone monuments
(cf. Liebers 1986). Attracted by such folklore and influenced by an emerging interest in history and a fascination with ancient ruins, Romantic
poets, painters, and travelers visited megaliths increasingly during the late
eighteenth and early nineteenth centuries. Among them was the landscape painter Caspar David Friedrich (1774–1840), whose work reflects
the enormous appeal megaliths held for him and his contemporaries as
picturesque remnants of a distant past. In the same spirit, the architects
of contemporaneous landscape parks, e.g., in Basedow and Burg Schlitz,
deliberately incorporated or imitated megalithic monuments in their cre-
ations, complementing their set of artificial ruins and other follies (see
Holtorf 2000–2004: 8.5, 8.6; cf. Woodward 2001).

Antiquarians and archaeologists have reopened and investigated
megaliths in large numbers since the nineteenth century. The sequence of
activities in Mecklenburg-Vorpommern is typical. A first generation of
archaeologists, including Friedrich Lisch (1801–1883) and Robert Beltz

(1854–1942), lobbied for and implemented legal protection of local archaeological monuments against their destruction by treasure hunters and stone robbers. Later, Ernst Sprockhoff (1892–1967) undertook a systematic survey, then published several large volumes containing a comprehensive collection of descriptions, plans, maps, and photographs. More recently, new research and excavation projects have been undertaken, mainly by Ewald Schuldt (1914–1987).

Today, many ancient monuments have become local attractions. In the tourist regions on Rügen and along the Baltic Sea, many archaeological sites are frequently visited during the summer months. Amateurs develop their own theories about the megaliths' true meanings. Artists use them for inspiration. In the light of so much attention, heritage managers are nowadays primarily concerned with the preservation, restoration, and presentation of ancient monuments. Sometimes it is therefore almost as if megaliths have died. After the completed autopsy, their bodies have been mummified and are displayed to the public, while the dates of their lives are published in obituaries.

On some occasions, monuments appear to behave more like zombies, for example, when "in a Frankenstein-like fashion" their "fragments were brought together, reinterpreted and re-assembled to create monuments which, although bearing little resemblance to the original, nevertheless took on a life of their own and began their biographies anew" (Moreland 1999: 209). After studying the twentieth-century restorations at the prehistoric sites of Avebury and Stonehenge in Britain, Brian Edwards (2000: 76) concludes similarly that "our ancient past is a ruination plundered by early antiquarians and despoiled by the heritage industry." This argument has attracted much public attention, but in light of this chapter's discussion, his findings do not necessarily have to be read as a criticism of modern changes to ancient sites. Every age has appropriated prehistoric monuments in its own way, and our own time is simply no exception. It is quite impossible either to recreate or to maintain a site as it originally was.

In sum it can be said that megaliths, like stone axes, are not merely of the Neolithic; they are invariably of all periods during which have they existed. Megaliths and stone axes may sometimes be treated as dead in our society, but it is a mistake to see them as such. They should rather be viewed analogously to historic buildings that have been occupied and used in different ways over many generations, often changing their functions and meanings but always maintaining a presence and a need to be interpreted. Today, public attention is often on archaeologists, who see megaliths both as clues for the academic study of the past and as manifestations of our cultural heritage. But whatever archaeologists do in relation to ancient sites and artifacts in the present, e.g., excavate, restore, display, or tell stories about them, can also be seen as simply their contribution to the *Geschichtskultur* of our age (cf. chapter 1).

Archaeologists' actions and perceptions are perhaps often particularly visible, but they are not the only contributions of our time to the lives of archaeological sites and artifacts. Next I must therefore consider a range of popular ways of knowing and appreciating ancient sites and objects and contextualize the archaeological perspective within them.

CHAPTER SIX
CONTEMPORANEOUS MEANINGS

People have been living in this town since the Stone Age. Proof for that is the seven meter tall Gollenstein which was erected here approximately four thousand years ago.

—Blieskastel, tourist leaflet (1993)

I n this chapter I review what archaeological sites mean to people in the present. As I show in the previous chapter, prehistoric stone monuments can be very impressive and evocative features of contemporary landscapes and have for many centuries attracted a wide range of responses. They are also particularly well suited to serve as examples for studying the wide variety of meanings of archaeological sites today (see also the case studies in Gazin-Schwartz and Holtorf 1999). Prehistoric monuments are places to visit and to spend time; they are educational as well as mystical; their images appear in leaflets, on postcards, and in a variety of books. Archaeological sites are enjoyed by some, avoided by others, and kept in order by others again. Such contemporary meanings of the remains of the past, as they are exemplified in the various receptions of archaeological monuments in the present landscape, are the topic of this chapter: how people make archaeological monuments intelligible and how they make sense and use of them.

In short, this chapter is about *Vorgeschichtskultur*, or "culture of prehistory" (adapting Rüsen's notion of *Geschichtskultur*, or "culture of history," as discussed in chapter 1). Such an investigation requires a specifically ethnographic approach. I will therefore draw on extensive ethnographic research about three German sites, which I conducted during the early 1990s. My case studies were of two standing stones (menhirs) of the early Bronze Age, one the Gollenstein in Blieskastel, Saarland (figure 6.1) and the other in Tübingen-Weilheim, Baden-Württemberg (figures 6.2 and 7.1), and of one Neolithic long barrow containing several megalithic grave chambers in Waabs-Karlsminde, Schleswig-Holstein. During my

Figure 6.1 The *Gollenstein* in Blieskastel, Saarland, Germany: sit down properly, enjoy, and learn. Photograph by Cornelius Holtorf, 1995.

research in the field, involving qualitative analyses of numerous documents, as well as questionnaires and interviews, I discerned fourteen different ways in which these sites are meaningful today. Just as the previous chapter includes a long-term account of the changing meanings of two categories of finds and sites, I draw here on a small sample of sites in order to illustrate the contemporary variety of meanings. The existing overlap between the various meanings demonstrates the many interdependencies between the categories discussed (see also Holtorf 2000–2004: 5.0).

Monumentality

Monumentality was what mattered most about the monuments to the first antiquarians. That is why they called these monuments "megaliths" ("large stones") or "menhirs" ("long stones"). Indeed, even today many people experience megalithic monuments mostly in terms of their sheer size and the huge weight of the stones used. At the Gollenstein, I asked a boy who was perhaps eight years old what he thought of the stone. He

Figure 6.2 The menhir of Tübingen-Weilheim, Baden-Württemberg, Germany. Wood engraving by Friederike von Redwitz, Weilheim (1991), reproduced by permission.

replied that he liked it "because it is so tall!" By the same token, the Gollenstein in fact is the largest menhir in central Europe and used to be mentioned as such in the *Guinness Book of World Records*. The information board at the long barrow of Karlsminde states that the monument is an amazing 60 meters long, 5.5 meters wide, and includes 108 stones weighing between 1.5 and 2.5 tons. Members of the group of volunteers who reconstructed the long barrow from 1976 to 1978 remember vividly how they had to cope with these truly monumental stones: "In the end we were so fit . . . our record was to erect eight stones on one day."

The outstanding visibility and dominant position of the large stones in the landscape is also what attracts people to go and look at megaliths. At Karlsminde, strollers, cyclists, or families traveling by car often spot the monument from a distance and then approach the site to have a look at it. Most visitors then walk around the monument once, read the information board provided, take a picture, and after three to five minutes, leave again. Local people, who are familiar with the site, also tend to head for specific places when out walking, and the long barrow is one such destination. The same goes for menhirs, which are particularly attractive also to dogs, which frequently leave their markings there when passing by on walks. Hence, a neighbor referred to the menhir in Weilheim as a *Pinkelstein* ("peeing stone"). Monuments can be targets also in another sense. The Gollenstein stood exactly on the German Westwall, the Siegfried Line. Being taller than 6.5 meters, it could easily have been used by hostile artillery as a point of orientation, thus illustrating once more the potential for monuments to change their meanings dramatically (see chapter 5). At the beginning of World War II, the menhir was therefore pushed over and as a result broke into four pieces. It was reerected in 1951. Today, amateur airplane pilots still employ clearly recognizable features in the landscape, like menhirs and megaliths, to orient themselves.

Factual Details

Professional archaeologists especially tend to consider prehistoric monuments as remains inherently containing scientific information about processes and events that took place in the past. Often, they emphasize such factual details: what it is, who discovered it, how large it is, how old it is, if there are any comparable finds elsewhere, and so on. A lot of people think that knowledge about an archaeological site necessarily appears in the form of such detailed information and scientific facts. Although considered boring by many, such facts are invariably also mentioned during guided tours, on leaflets and information boards, in documentary reports in the media, and in lessons taught about the monuments in schools. An astonishing number of visitors seem fully satisfied with the site after having subjected themselves to reading such details. Some can never get enough information about whatever little detail, as some quotes from my questionnaires and interviews illustrate: "I am interested in everything"; "I want to know everything which I don't know already"; "there are thousands of questions which make one suffer, somehow." Indeed, amateur archaeologists are sometimes able to provide their professional counterparts with new details and information about known sites or even to find new ones.

Perhaps unsurprisingly, archaeologists are often perceived as knowing the factual details best and, thus, as the most important scholarly experts

95

concerning ancient sites. Indeed, some were confused when I asked them about the meaning of a monument. Even regarding their own perspectives, they seemingly preferred to rely on experts: "Since you study this, you should know the answers!" Amateur archaeologists sometimes try to convince their professional colleagues of the quality of their own work by imitating even the dry and unimaginative writing style found in so many academic works offering scientific expertise. Similarly, in order to impress me with their knowledge, some of my interviewees had obviously made an effort to memorize some supposedly basic facts (dates, measurements, technical terms). Factual details thus acquire metaphorical significance and are used to display conformity with perceived educational values and to express desired social distinctions (see Schulze 1993: 142–50).

Commerce

Archaeology and prehistoric monuments as a part of the archaeological heritage have proven both popular and commercially exploitable (cf. Kristiansen 1993). Some sites, although not those among my case studies, charge entrance fees. Business people can also make profits selling archaeological merchandise, such as postcards showing the local monuments like those for sale at the camping ground in Karlsminde and throughout the town of Blieskastel. Furthermore, the Gollenstein features on tiles, beer mugs, drinking glasses, egg cups, and so forth. A large oil company once offered to sponsor a rose tree at the Gollenstein in order to boost its regional image. In a similar effort, the local bank of Blieskastel distributed bottle openers in the shape of the Gollenstein.

Monuments are also important as factors stimulating the economy of the area in which they are situated (cf. Liebers 1986: chapter 11; Schörken 1995: chapter 4.2). In the mid-1970s the economic situation in Waabs was such that it required an additional attraction for tourists. The former mayor explained the situation to me:

> What do we have to offer here? We make guests come here and advertise with brochures. We advertise with the Baltic Sea, with the beach, and with our landscape. But not only those people come here who lie on the beach from morning to evening. They also want to get to know the countryside and the people. And what can they visit here? The

church of Waabs used to be all we had. Now [the reconstructed long barrow of] Karlsminde has been added. (My translation[1])

Bus tours to Karlsminde now even come from Denmark. Investing money in the preservation and restoration of archaeological monuments thus attracts heritage tourism and brings money into the local community. Not surprisingly, images of prehistoric monuments appear widely in tourist advertising material and in travel guides.

Social Order

The various receptions of monuments are in many ways mirrors of the present. Interpretations of megaliths are often linked to contemporary assumptions, associations, and analogies and are subject to changing social policies and fashions. References to common stereotypes make sites popular and economically successful (see chapter 8). Our own social order is perhaps most visible and enforced at occasions like opening ceremonies such as those that took place at the restored Gollenstein in Blieskastel in 1951, at the reconstructed long barrow in Karlsminde in 1978, and at the new replica of the menhir in Weilheim in 1989. These rituals usually consist of a performance by a musical band, followed by several speeches given by political dignitaries and representatives of appropriate archaeological institutions, eventually leading to an extensive informal party with food and drinks provided. In Karlsminde even Gerhard Stoltenberg, then prime minister of the state of Schleswig-Holstein and a leading member of the Christian Democrat Party at the national level, came to open the megalithic tomb to the public.

Another example of the extent to which contemporary social norms and values dominate the meaning of monuments is provided by what is considered their proper reception. The geographer Tim Cresswell (1996: chapter 4) demonstrated how the conflicts over recent decades at Stone-

---

1. German original: "Was haben wir denn hier anzubieten? Wir holen die Fremden her, werben mit Prospekten. Wir werben mit der Ostsee, mit dem Strand und mit unserer Landschaft. Aber es kommen ja nicht nur Leute, die sich hier an den Strand legen von morgens bis abends. Die wollen ja auch Land und Leute kennenlernen. Und denn, was können wir hier besichtigen, nicht? Ja, die Waabser Kirche—das war's eigentlich, was wir hier hatten. Und nun ist [das rekonstruierte Langbett von] Karlsminde hinzugekommen."

henge were ultimately based on different social values held by the conservative government under Margaret Thatcher and the free festivalers and their supporters (see chapter 5). Whereas the government portrayed itself as the protector of moderate middle-class citizens against lawless hippies, some festivalers in turn saw themselves as the better people, who cared for preservation, nature, and spirituality.

According to the values of the educated middle classes, which governments and their agencies tend to make their own, archaeological sites have to be in order, i.e., they have to conform to certain expectations. The grass around the monument should be cut. A bench is where visitors are supposed to sit and enjoy. Bins are provided for any waste, and they have to be emptied regularly: no decay must be visible in any form. The information board is written by the experts and lets you know what you need to know. The visitor's interpretation of the monument has to be in order as well: what differs from standard interpretations runs the danger of being mocked and dismissed in public as *Schnickschnack* ("twaddle"). If you conform to expectations, you display your high-level education and culture.

There are also orders of research. Archaeologists study the past according to the rules and norms of academic discourse (cf. Shanks 1990; Tilley 1990). Often they have to comply not only with unwritten laws about the ownership of particular bodies of material in order to gain the cooperation of their colleagues but also with strict rules of how archaeological material has to be analyzed and interpreted in order for their manuscripts to be accepted in particular academic journals or book series. Sometimes amateurs are not taken seriously by professional archaeologists for the reason that they do not have academic titles in front of their names or an institution behind them. Significantly, the then state archaeologist of Schleswig-Holstein stated in a letter to me that "asking a state archaeologist what a megalithic tomb means to him is like asking the pope what the Catholic Church means to him." In this view, the state archaeologist is defined by his relation to the monuments and considered as being firmly in control of them, while possibly being infallible in matters of belief and judgment. Alternative claims to archaeological monuments are effectively treated as heresy. How we interpret and deal with monuments and with the past in general depends, then, greatly on their metaphorical significance and has to a considerable extent to do with social power.

Monument preservation, too, is part of our social order. Insofar as it follows from specific laws, it can even be enforced by the police. At the worst, heavy fines or even jail sentences may result from serious offences against such laws. People have thus become cautious about alarming the authorities. A resident of Weilheim had noticed the large menhir on the building site where it was found for several weeks but preferred not to report it. She said, "Well, I thought, it's better not to interfere, it's not your business. Don't cause a stir, they might start digging and who knows what else." She described what happened when archaeologists eventually discovered the menhir after being tipped off by somebody else: "the two [pre-historians] went straight to the mayor and confiscated the stone, as it were. This impressed me somehow: a stone which lay there unnoticed for months, and now suddenly it was important, at this moment on the record, officially protected."

Remembrance

Monuments, as memorials, also remind (mostly) local people of events that have taken place in that area many years before. Inhabitants of Blieskastel associate the Gollenstein with the time when they were children: "I spent my childhood in its vicinity"; "I grew up with it as a child and I have known it forever"; "as children we went up there to play." Some elderly people remembered World War II when I asked them for the meaning of the menhir: they still think of the Siegfried line running there. An ex-soldier had especially vivid memories of the monument:

> When we as soldiers were on leave home and the train approached Blieskastel, we could see the Gollenstein first. Later, when it lay broken, it was a dreadful feeling: the symbol of Blieskastel! And when I returned from captivity I had to fall in line up there and help to put things back in order. (My translation[2])

The restoration and reconstruction campaign at Karlsminde in the late 1970s, as well as the opening ceremonies of all three monuments,

---

2. German original: "Wenn man als Soldat Heimaturlaub hatte und kam dann mit dem Zug von Bierbach runtergefahren, Richtung Blieskastel, dann sah man halt den Gollenstein. Wie er zerbrochen war, das war natürlich ein greuliches Gefühl: das Wahrzeichen von Blieskastel! Und wie ich dann als Soldat, d.h. aus Gefangenschaft, zurückkam, mußte ich da oben antreten und helfen, die Sache in Ordnung zu bringen."

stayed in people's minds for a long time too. In Karlsminde, locals recall the fact that the prime minister of Schleswig-Holstein attended; in Weilheim a couple remembered that "it was a very turbulent festival" back in 1989. Prehistoric monuments also remind some visitors of other archaeological sites they have seen abroad while on holidays. People from elsewhere, in turn, remember their stays in Karlsminde, Weilheim, or Blieskastel when they look at their photographs showing the local prehistoric monument. In addition, some visitors leave visible traces behind at monuments, such as graffiti, in order to remind others and themselves of their visit. By carving their initials and the year (or whatever else) into the stone, they hope to render the monument into a memorial of their visit and of themselves, hence gaining "nominal immortality" (Lowenthal 1985: 331).

> **Thesis 8:**
> Archaeological sites mean very different things to different people, and these meanings are equally important.

Identities

A relation to the past is crucial to people's identities (Lowenthal 1985: 41–46). Prehistoric monuments in particular can serve as powerful emotional foci for both personal and collective identities and thus become a metaphor for yet another thing.

For example, a megalith might be considered to represent somebody's personal identity. The woman who first recognized the menhir of Weilheim considers this stone as her own life's work; she is convinced that if she dies the menhir may be what remains of her life. This may also be the reason others feel inspired to carve their initials in monuments such as the Gollenstein. For the amateur archaeologists who took part in the restoration and reconstruction of the long barrow of Karlsminde, the monument became an important part of their life histories and identities, too; one of them called it even "my baby." In Blieskastel, one amateur archaeologist set up a miniature park of menhirs and dolmens in his back garden, and the same man sells hand-carved wooden Gollensteins for little money at local flea markets. Somebody else feels so close to the same menhir that he calls the stone "my friend." A couple of years ago an artist planned an installation involving the Gollenstein in order to "get into the stone and to melt together my innermost part with it." This project has never been carried out though. Amateur researchers may spend years of their lives and large proportions of their savings on trips to archaeological sites around the globe in order to write new accounts of the past. But professional archaeologists, too, see ancient monuments sometimes as much more than objects of study; they feel and care for them, and they even like spending their holidays and retirement age in their occasional company. Archaeological work can thus become very personal indeed (cf. Shanks 1992: 130–31).

Collective identities can also be connected with archaeological monuments. People have always identified themselves with the place or area in which they are living, and they are generally proud of its heritage, often eager to show "their" antiquities to visitors. Another factor has now been added. The faster the world we live in changes, with people feeling increasingly alienated from the actual bases of their lives, the more we may come to draw on the past as heritage for a compensating reassurance about who we actually are (cf. Nora 1989). Ancient sites can become symbols of common roots and a communal spirit that binds a community together (see Schörken 1995: 111–12, 127). This community may be the village where the monument is situated, the nearest town, a district, a region, a state, or an entire nation.

Even a monument that has only recently been dug up is rapidly considered to be part of "our past." In Weilheim people are proud that their own village with a menhir from the early Bronze Age is ostensibly older than the neighboring Kilchberg, which has "only" a reconstructed burial mound of the Iron Age. Inhabitants of Alschbach, which today is part of the town of Blieskastel, jokingly still claim the Gollenstein as theirs because it stands on what used to be their land. Even so, the town of Blieskastel now happily advertises with the phrase "attractive for 4,000 years" (see also the quotation at the beginning of this chapter). There is also a lot of local pride about having "Germany's tallest menhir" in the small town of Blieskastel. In the summer the entire town celebrates the annual *Gollensteinfest*. Posters of the Gollenstein can be found in many local shop windows, and one person admitted to me that she also has a poster of it hanging above her own bed. The menhir is also used as a name for a local travel agency, *Gollenstein-Reisen*.

Moving on from the local to the regional level, it is significant that in his six-page speech script for the opening ceremony in Karlsminde, the prime minister of Schleswig-Holstein managed to include the name of his state no less than fifteen times, the word for "state" was used another fifteen times, and eleven references were made to *Heimat* (which refers to a very strong sense of belonging to a community and its traditions). Thereby, Prime Minister Stoltenberg reassured people about where they belong at the same time that he linked himself, the government, and his party with the regional identity of the area. By the same token, in the Saarland all children in their final year of primary school (at the age of 10) take a trip around their state. The Gollenstein has traditionally been a part of the itinerary because it is seen as a monument of key significance to the children's *Heimat*. To refer publicly, when at prehistoric monuments in Germany, to a common national past is rare and widely considered as a form of unapproved nationalism (see Schmidt and Halle 1999), but the equivalent is common in other states such as Denmark (see Kristiansen 1993). In one instance I encountered a notion of universal human identity: a woman considered the menhir of Weilheim as part of the "history of mankind."

Ancient sites can also come to stand for various social identities. Perhaps most visible to archaeologists is the meaning they acquire for them themselves. The long barrow of Karlsminde, for example, is often presented to visiting archaeologists or conference participants as some kind of shop sign or showpiece for local archaeology. Unsurprisingly, the group of volunteers who originally restored the site had also developed a strong bond to the site that effectively defined their relationship to each other. Monuments can be important foci for nonarchaeologists too, as the various documented communities interested in Stonehenge illustrate (see Chippindale et al. 1990; Cresswell 1996: chapter 4). Among my case studies, the Gollenstein, for example, is known as a place where local youths meet occasionally for nocturnal parties, seemingly deriding the venerable monument.

Aesthetics

A lot of people come to see megaliths because they enjoy the scenery and the aesthetics of prehistoric monuments. Ancient ruins partly decayed and grown over have long inspired the Western imagination (figure 4.3; see also Lowenthal 1985: chapter 4; Woodward 2001). It is therefore not surprising that ancient sites in the landscape often feature prominently in tourist brochures, as mentioned before.

Ancient monuments evoke a particular form of romanticism, and they are often especially appreciated at sundown. For example, a neighbor of the menhir in Weilheim stated, "Sometimes it is so lovely when we experience sunsets here—I can well imagine that they practiced a cult of the sun here at certain times." In many cases, such impressions are intensified by the monument's remoteness and the tranquility and beauty of the surrounding landscape. A brochure about Eckernförde, from which Karlsminde is within convenient driving distance, observes that "the charm of the rural atmosphere is impressed by millennia and preserved in its origin." Both amateur and professional photographers regularly visit monuments in order to take pictures capturing this atmosphere. School parties draw them in class after joint visits. Even oil paintings of archaeological sites in the landscape are occasionally produced, continuing a genre that was first made popular by romantic painters like Caspar David Friedrich.

Reflections

A monument's age encourages people to reflect upon themselves and the world in philosophical terms. It seems as if the presence of a witness from the past can quite easily evoke profound existential reflections, for instance about the course of time, death, and decay, and the hopes and values by which we live today. Deep thoughts I came across include the following:

> When I see this stone I know that I stand on ground that is historically eminent, where already in 2000 BC a lot happened. To me, [the monument] is the visualization of a spirit which is transmitted through the generations.
>
> The Gollenstein is a venerable witness of the past. . . . In its stony tranquillity . . . the Gollenstein is a reminder for us of the transitoriness of all human doings as well as of the insignificance of the daily arguing about trifles.
>
> Sometimes I get the impression that many contemporaries, in terms of religion, beliefs, etc., live very superficially. I think that perhaps such an old stone may also encourage certain reflections: why did they build

it? Then I have secretly the very tiny hope that people may also ask themselves: Well, what do I stick to in my own life? (My translations[3])

Adventures

People visit archaeological sites in their leisure time, seeking special experiences that can, for instance, be gained by visiting exotic curiosities and strange wonders. That is precisely what many prehistoric monuments offer: they are very huge, very old, and very extraordinary. As metaphors for the strange, they stimulate people to feel extraordinary, too (see Köck 1990; cf. Schulze 1993). This inspiration is one aspect of what I will call the "archaeo-appeal" of ancient sites and artifacts (see chapter 9).

There are two main kinds of adventurous archaeology signified by archaeological monuments. One is the encounter with an exciting and adventurous past. Such a past is often depicted in images of (pre-)historic life but has ultimately more to do with certain needs and desires of the present. American archaeologist J. M. Fritz (1973: 75–76) writes about the appeal of the prehistory of Arizona to the "common man":

> The vicarious but safe experience of the drama implicit or explicit from archaeological accounts of the invasions; the movements of people; the burning and looting of towns; the revolutionary transformations; the interplay of priests, rulers, and warrior castes; or simply the day-to-day exertions of living and of "man the hunter" are undoubtedly related to deeply felt needs. . . . For such men [and women] and perhaps for us, the past is an empty stage to be filled with actors and actions dictated

---

3. German originals:

"Wenn ich diesen Stein hier sehe, dann weiß ich, daß ich auf einem Boden stehe, der geschichtsträchtig ist, wo hier also schon 2000 vor Christus einiges passiert ist. Es ist für mich die Sichtbarmachung dieses Geistes, der sich eben so durch die Generationen fortpflanzt."

"Der Gollenstein ist ein ehrwürdiger Zeuge der Vergangenheit. . . . In seiner steinernen Ruhe . . . ist uns der Gollenstein ein Mahnmal für die Vergänglichkeit allen menschlichen Tuns und für die Bedeutungslosigkeit des täglichen Streitens um Nichtigkeiten."

"Ich habe manchmal den Eindruck, daß viele Zeitgenossen doch sehr oberflächlich leben, was Religion, Glaube usw. angeht. Und da denke ich, daß auch so ein alter Stein zum Nachdenken anregt: weshalb haben die das gemacht? Da habe ich dann insgeheim die ganz kleine Hoffnung, daß die Leute sich dann fragen: Ja, also woran halte ich mich eigentlich?"

by our needs and desires. For individuals, the past provides escape . . .
and opportunity to produce good and evil and to create and thus control
events we most desire or fear. In this sense, the past is an extension of
dreams and daydreams.

Donald Duck has been known, too, to long for "adventure—the kind of
rip-snorting fun those old Vikings must have had!" Consequently, he
embarked on precisely one such adventure, chasing the golden helmet (see
Service 1998a).

These kinds of connotations of the past may also be the reason why
certain feasts and ceremonies are held at some ancient sites nowadays. In
Blieskastel, the annual summer *Gollensteinfest* has proven extremely popular since it was first established in 1971. On that particular weekend,
almost the entire town gathers around the Gollenstein, and people enjoy
themselves while eating, drinking, and dancing to live music. Occasionally, smaller and more private feasts are held at the Gollenstein as well: I
was told about a Beltane festival, an American Indian fancy-dress party,
an end-of-excavation party, and a party of acolytes of local parishes, as
well as several Whitsuntide scout jamborees and numerous feasts of local
clubs and groups of youths with campfires and freely flowing alcohol.

Whereas archaeological monuments like menhirs and megaliths may
once have been positioned in places that were (or became) special and
different from those normally frequented, nowadays they derive much of
their special appeal from the different time period they are associated
with. Many people, including children, love speculating about what went
on at such monuments during prehistory. In popular books and media
productions, as well as in the opinions of some of my interviewees, prehistoric monuments are interpreted as astronomic observatories, as places of
ancestor or sun worship, magic ritual, fertility cults, human sacrifice, and
cannibalism, as well as seats of chiefs, princes, or kings, and so on. It
seems that the stranger, the better (cf. Schmidt and Halle 1999). In a
similar spirit, the megaliths of Schleswig-Holstein are also known as the
pyramids of the North. Likewise, menhirs are not infrequently associated
with the comic figure Obelix, who supposedly as a small child fell into a
pot of magic potion brewed by the local druid, giving him superhuman
strength and the ability constantly to carry a menhir on his back. Extraordinary goings on at monuments are also told of in legends and fables that
still surround many prehistoric sites (see Grinsell 1976; Liebers 1986).

People enjoy reliving the excitements of the past. Few things, for instance, are as popular as prehistoric flint-knapping demonstrations. When (pre-)historic events are reenacted, everyday life is relived, or ancient technologies are tested by experiment, these extraordinary and exciting activities as such appear to attract people (cf. Schörken 1995: 134–37; Gustafsson 2002). One recent study (Hjemdahl 2002: 111) showed that even peeling carrots can be experienced as fun as long as you are "in the past"!

Sometimes, reliving (pre-)history can enable the unfulfilled wishes and desires of the present to become true by projecting them onto the past. The Swedish archaeologist Bodil Petersson (2003: 339–46) demonstrated how reconstructions and reenactments of different periods have appeals for people with different lifestyles and desires. The Stone Age offers a happy, egalitarian, and ecological idyll involving all sorts of simple technical skills; the Bronze Age is more hierarchical and adds cosmology, ritual, and cult issues, which suit those inspired by New Age ideas; families with children are attracted to daily life in the Iron Age, characterized by farming and breeding livestock; the Viking age is often male oriented, involving heroes on ships, traders in markets, and visitors to festivals; the Middle Ages, finally, have even more markets and festivals, especially tournaments, and are full of knights, merchants, and nobility, with everybody playing very clearly defined roles.

A second kind of adventurous archaeology is the idea of archaeology as an adventurous endeavor in itself. In this view, archaeologists are handsome adventurers who lead dangerous lives on the trail of treasure in foreign countries (see chapter 3). Some sort of special excitement about archaeology was certainly required by the volunteers who worked in their leisure time over several years at the reconstruction of the long barrow of Karlsminde.

Aura

Prehistoric monuments are authentic witnesses of bygone times (see chapter 7). They emanate aura and cosmic atmosphere. A visitor to Karlsminde thus enjoyed the site of the reconstructed long barrow for it allowed him "to let his soul swing." One man I met in Blieskastel claimed to be able to "see the aura" of the restored Gollenstein and enjoyed being there at night or during the early hours of the morning. Its aura was ostensibly unaffected after the site had been restored and renovated. Indeed, restoring, reconstructing, or maintaining an ancient monument is often the result of a particularly deeply felt admiration, respect, and even reverence for the past and its remains. At the opening ceremony of the long barrow at Waabs-Karlsminde, the local mayor declared in this vein, "We bow down in great respect before those who constructed this monument." Moving any such site away from its current position might thus destroy the aura of the monument.

When I asked the head of the municipal cultural authority in Blieskastel why he would not want to put a copy in the place of the Gollenstein, which is jeopardized by environmental pollution, he replied, "Somehow, it wouldn't be the same. . . . This wouldn't be an appropriate thing to do." This concern was borne out when the original menhir of Weilheim was moved to the museum in the state capital, Stuttgart, and replaced by a replica (see chapter 7). In addition, not long after the replica was inaugurated in 1989, a fire hydrant and several brightly painted posts were placed right in front of the menhir. Not much of an aura or much sense of authenticity is now perceptible there. Every visitor instantly discovers the replica at the very latest when knocking against it: "It sounds like a plastic watering can," one local said. People thus experience the menhir as "made of plastic" and a "fake." In a local publication Ute Jönsson expressed a more widely felt desire in asking rhetorically, "Who does not want to touch at least once the original daggers [which adorn the menhir] with his or her own hand?"

Magical Places

A lot of people are attracted by a somewhat magical mystery that surrounds ancient monuments. Some see menhirs in general as places of magical practices performed by fertility cults and as phallic symbols. Interestingly enough, some elderly inhabitants of Blieskastel remember well that the Gollenstein also used to be the target of various Easter processions from the surrounding villages. At the beginning of the last century, a little niche was cut into the monument and may have been filled with a saint's figurine. Perhaps this was an effort to Christianize the site physically as well. Even today, quite a few pilgrims who come to Blieskastel as a place of Roman Catholic pilgrimage visit the Gollenstein afterwards. As a matter of fact, it is very difficult to get people talking about anything that could be considered superstitious or occult because the public discourse in our society tends to disapprove of any such affinities. Usually only evidence for lovers' rendezvous at monuments is found or given, but even this may be significant. An elderly woman, after I had asked her for her associations with the Gollenstein, said, "Well, what do we think there? We ought not to reveal it at all. Once in May, we were young— then we often went up there."

During the night of the summer solstice in 1993, a couple of teenagers appeared at the Gollenstein and put a candle in a small niche of the menhir. I asked one of them why they came there on that day, and I was given the following information: "I knew, in Stonehenge etc., there is always something going on [during this night]. I expected that there would be some people here. And, of course, I have been joking all the time that you get sacrifices of virgins here on that day" (My translation[4]).

Such jokes certainly refer to, and further popularize, interpretations of monuments as places where magical practices once took place and sacrifices were offered to the gods. Although there is thus some affinity in the present with the magic of monuments, it is not always entirely serious. A local vicar said that he would think that "the people are pagan in other ways than that." The local police station in Blieskastel could not provide any evidence for pagan rituals at the Gollenstein either. But another person I met had an idea to celebrate pagan weddings at the Gollenstein. He considered such rituals at that place as an appropriate alternative to what the dominant, Christian church is performing nowadays. One reason for this may be that prehistoric monuments are occasionally seen as places where sacred forces of nature can be experienced (see Chippindale et al. 1990: chapter 2; Shanks 1992: 59–63; Schmidt and Halle 1999).

There are special techniques that allow some of us to sense the force fields of the earth, which are related to its magnetic and electrical fields. They usually employ various kinds of rods. According to these somewhat esoteric approaches, monuments were built at locations where such fields

---

4. German original: "Ich wußte, bei Stonehenge und so ist ja auch immer was los. Ich habe erwartet, daß hier irgendwelche Leute sind. Und ich mache natürlich ständig auch meine blöden Scherzen so, daß da Jungfrauenopferungen wären an dem Tag hier und so."

are strongest, often along the ridges of hills. There is a connection here to the famous ley-lines, i.e., alignments of ancient sites stretching across the landscape, because such forces are believed to be responsible for the human organization of the landscape in general, resulting in sacred geometries. Often, monuments are sites where some can sense such underlying powers of nature, known as "Earth mysteries." As one person I spoke to put it, it is possible at such locations "to fill up with energy." The same man spends a lot of time at the Gollenstein "opening [himself] to Truth and endless Love." It is sometimes assumed that the druids were especially capable of experiences such as this and developed around them a secret knowledge of nature. In some people's views, we should aim at regaining such insights in order to understand better not only the ancient monuments but also the world in which we are living now.

Nostalgia

Following a nostalgic view of the past, some find the past, for instance the Neolithic, more attractive to live in than the present because "in yesterday we find what we miss today" (Lowenthal 1985: 49). People of the past were allegedly more open to the spiritual and to cosmic vibrations in the landscape: they were less strongly rooted in the material. About the Gollenstein I was told, "The past humans lived in an even and stable context. All tensions and contradictions were ultimately reconciled." A resident of Weilheim stated that in the past "all was of one piece. Everybody knew what to do and what to believe. The world was like this and that was it." Somebody else said, "humans then also did not take themselves as so important." For others again, prehistoric people lived in harmony with their fellow humans and with nature: "People then were more reasonable" than we are today, as someone put it in conversation. In this view, we should try to reach this state again in order to save the human race and indeed the entire world from evil. Supposedly, people in the past also lived idyllically, "less hectically," and in harmony with nature because "everything was nature then." At the same time, people were not at all primitive but "as intelligent as we are": "they had all the ancient monuments after all."

Many difficult problems we are confronted with today did not exist several millennia ago: there was no pollution of the environment, no danger of another world war, and no traffic either. A schoolgirl wrote on one of my questionnaires, "Given all that you hear now in the news—I would rather have been on earth during a former age!" Life used to be just nice; simply "everything was better." An archaeologist told me that he, too, wished he had lived in an earlier age

> because then the ways of warfare, for instance, were much more humane really, if you think about it. Today you can be as strong and clever as you want—in a war you would be lost. . . . In former times strength, aptitude, and reason were still in the foreground. They are after all essential virtues of human beings. (My translation[5])

Progress

According to the opposite view of the past, the past was primitive and not worthy of reliving, whereas our future in fact depends on continuous progress. The human beings who built the monuments are considered to have been backward and poorly developed culturally because they did not yet have many of the later inventions of modern civilizations. They used hand axes and wore furs, "hunted foxes and rabbits in the forest," and lived in caves without any heating, except their campfires. Life must have been difficult: "they did not have an Aldi [supermarket] then, and they had to make sure they would survive the winter." One schoolgirl stated, "The humans were poorer in former times and I do not approve of that." They also did not have doctors or dentists. Life was therefore continuously put at risk by disease and, what is worse, by slavery. A woman in Blieskastel admitted to me that if she had lived in the past she would have been constantly afraid of being burnt as a witch.

Progress is supposedly obvious in the history of archaeology, too. Educational curricula and the media tend to make much of the continuous progress of the sciences, and archaeology is seen as one of them. Most scientific archaeologists are indeed explicitly working towards this aim.

---

5. German original: "weil dort zum Beispiel die Art und Weise der Kriegsführung viel humaner war eigentlich, wenn ich das so betrachte. Heute können Sie so stark und so schlau sein wie Sie wollen—in einem Krieg sind Sie verloren. . . . Früher, da stand noch Kraft, Geschicklichkeit und Verstand im Vordergrund. Das sind ja wesentliche Tugenden des Menschen."

The history of the discipline has been written as a story of continually improving our knowledge about the past, although other views are equally possible (see Schnapp 1996). This may explain why so many people rely happily on the expertise of archaeologists as scientific specialists. It could be argued, however, that this notion is self-serving since it secures the archaeologists' social status and justifies their claim to intellectual control over the past.

Ideologies

Certain qualities ascribed to the past or to monuments are ideological in the sense that they legitimize particular social and political claims or interests (see also Tilley 1989a). By signifying the distant human past, archaeological sites have an important metaphorical potential, which may become ideological when supposedly reflecting how best to act and think "naturally." Changing explanations for past events and processes can reveal in retrospect how every generation of scholars had its own explanatory factors that offered themselves naturally, giving answers that were plausible at the time because they related to dominant ideologies and common ways of interpreting the world (see Wilk 1985). Both nostalgia and progress can have strong ideological dimensions in that they seem to point to a better way of life that will, however, suit some contemporary needs better than others.

All these various meanings are given to the prehistoric monuments I investigated, signifying various aspects and dimensions of contemporary knowledge about the past and its material remains. They illustrate how ancient sites can function as metaphors for a wide range of meanings and values. These results of my fieldwork, although no more than a first attempt to come to terms with the contemporary meanings of prehistoric monuments, raise some important questions. If interpretations and meanings of archaeological objects vary to the extent shown, depending on the particular viewpoint and interest of the observer in each present, where does that leave the very materiality and the authenticity of genuine artifacts? Can the aura of the original remain unaffected when everything else is in motion?

AUTHENTICITY

> In principle it is possible for any new-fangled gimmick, which at one point appeared to be nothing but a staged "tourist trap," to become over time, and under appropriate conditions, widely recognized as an "authentic" manifestation of local culture.
>
> —Eric Cohen (1988: 380)

The previous two chapters illustrate how the meaning of ancient monuments is largely dependent on who is looking at them in what context. This raises the question whether there is an essential core of a site or, indeed, artifact that is embedded in its very materiality, ensuring its authenticity, and not subject to change depending on the observer. Or is there nothing that distinguishes precious originals from worthless copies? Can a site or artifact that has been materially restored, reconstructed, or in other ways manufactured retain its authenticity?

In this and the following chapter I argue that more important than the actual age of a site or artifact is its perceived "pastness," i.e., the way it allows the past to be experienced. This argument requires first a reappreciation of the concept of authenticity.

What Is Authenticity?

The notion of authenticity is a product of Western cultural history with roots in antiquity (cf. Jokilehto 1995; Petzet 1995). While the term itself derives from the Greek *authentikòs*, containing *autòs* ("same") and, thus, denoting a relation of identity with itself, its modern meaning was largely defined by the romantics and their contemporaries in the later eighteenth and early nineteenth centuries. Since then, authenticity has been taken to mean a condition of an object that can be revealed insofar as it exists but cannot be willfully created. Authenticity is what distinguishes an original and unique work of art from a mechanical reproduction, giving it credibility and authority (Benjamin 1992). Later the concept of authenticity was extended from art objects to folklore and traditions and even to entire landscapes.

In relation to ancient art and monuments, authenticity has usually been understood as the material integrity of the object itself. Since Johann Joachim Winckelmann (1717–1768), the father of classical archaeology, it has been a generally accepted rule that (the remains of) ancient objects should be conserved and preserved, rather then restored, renovated, or reconstructed, and that modern repairs, where they are necessary, must not distort the overall impression and ought to be clearly distinguishable from the authentic remains themselves. Although not unchallenged, this line was later reaffirmed by art historians like Georg Dehio (1850–1932) with his slogan, "Conserve, do not restore." Another famous art historian, the Austrian Alois Riegl (1858–1905) noted in his famous essay "The Modern Cult of Monuments" (1982 [1903]) that the "historical value" of ancient monuments as original remains of the past is opposed to their "age-value" resulting from traces of disintegration and decay. From the standpoint of age-value, there is no need to worry about the eternal preservation of monuments; instead, their authenticity lies in the process of natural decay and gradual vanishing. In an attempt to reconcile the two values, Riegl pointed out not only that age-value partly depends on historical value, but that it may even justify some preservational efforts, for instance against premature decay or deliberate destruction of a monument. Today, an ethic of conservation and preservation is virtually universally accepted. After it was put into words in 1964 in the International Charter for the Conservation and Restoration of Monuments and Sites, also known as the Venice Charter, the same values found their way into numerous national legislations concerning ancient sites and objects around the world, for better or worse (cf. Byrne 1991).

In recent years, a true cult of authenticity has emerged where virtually any object is to be conserved and preserved in its authenticity: from "authentic smells" to "authentic wooden lard beaters" (Lowenthal 1994: 37–40). Even people can be described as being authentic and therefore worth knowing. Despite this popularity of the term *authenticity*, there is considerable conceptual confusion as to what it actually means. This has become a problem for institutions such as the UNESCO World Heritage Centre and the International Council of Monuments and Sites

(ICOMOS), which are in the business of evaluating whether particular ancient sites are authentic or not. While the term originally referred to the genuineness of the material and some of its properties (e.g., design, workmanship), such a relatively narrow concept of authenticity, it is widely felt, neither allows enough flexibility for special circumstances in the Western world nor does justice to non-Western traditions of valuing ancient sites. In order to discuss this matter fully and come to an appropriate definition of authenticity that could be applied worldwide, two UNESCO-sponsored conferences were organized and later published. The results of these meetings were expressed in the "Nara Document on Authenticity" (Larsen 1995: xxi–xxv). Paragraphs 11 and 13 of that document make the following interesting statements:

> All judgements about values attributed to heritage as well as the credibility of related information sources may differ from culture to culture, and even within the same culture. It is thus not possible to base judgements of value and authenticity on fixed criteria. On the contrary, the respect due to all cultures requires that cultural heritage must be considered and judged within the cultural contexts to which it belongs.
>
> Depending on the nature of the cultural heritage, its cultural context, and its evolution through time, authenticity judgements may be linked to the worth of a great variety of sources of information. Aspects of these sources may include form and design, materials and substance, use and function, traditions and techniques, location and setting, and spirit and feeling, and other internal and external factors. The use of these sources permits elaboration of the specific artistic, historic, social and scientific dimensions of the cultural heritage being examined. (Larsen 1995: xxiii)

In appendix II of the document, "information sources" are defined as "all material, written, oral and figurative sources which make it possible to know the nature, specifications, meaning and history of the cultural heritage" (Larsen 1995: xxv). In effect this means that authenticity can mean many different things in different cultural contexts. A monument may be considered authentic not only if it closely resembles an ancient structure in form and design but also if its spirit and feeling are those of an ancient building (for good examples, see Stille 2002: chapter 2; Lowenthal 1995).

Experiencing Aura and Authenticity

Despite the theoretical difficulties in defining it, authenticity is arguably the single most important property of archaeological finds and exhibits. Having studied two British heritage attractions, Gaynor Bagnall (1996: 241) notes that in her visitor sample "authenticity was considered extremely important and was to some extent used as a legitimization for the visit." Although we may never be able to see artifacts on display in the same way in which they were seen by their makers, there was nevertheless a clear desire "for the experience to be based in fact, to be genuine."

This experience of authenticity has sometimes been described as the experience of an "aura" of an original. According to Walter Benjamin in his classic paper "The Work of Art in the Age of Mechanical Reproduction" (1992), aura is a property that resides in genuine artifacts and distinguishes originals from mechanical reproductions. Aura is thus the form in which age and authenticity can supposedly be sensed from the object itself. Accordingly, referring to Benjamin, Michael Shanks (1998: 20) states, "Aura is not a quality which people bring to something," but it is the "attribute" of an object, resulting from its previous life history. The perceived temporal distance between past and present suddenly melts away at the moment of discovery (see chapter 2), when the digger realizes that the very last person to touch the object just recovered lived several hundreds or thousands of years ago (e.g., Pallottino 1968: 11). This is perhaps the moment when the aura of the authentic find becomes most apparent. A good example is from the field diary of Britt Arnesen (2001) when she describes the moment of finding an obsidian microblade (see also sidebar):

> I am stunned, rendered motionless in my awed shock for a few seconds until I gingerly pick it up with my fingertips, and clean off the dirt in my palm. The sun catches it and dances through the colourless crystal. . . . So here I am, holding this powerful piece of technology, the last evidence of the ingenuity and versatility of the human mind. I fight my reverent silence until I am finally able to let out a gasped, "Wow . . ."

Britt Arnesen had found a piece of antiquity itself, emanating a powerful aura. Underlying her experiences and hidden in the assumption that

An Artifact of the Dune People
(from the field diary of Britt Arnesen)

I looked at the ground as if it had something to say to me. I asked it questions like "How are you today?" and "How does it feel to be trodden for the first time in years?" I was shocked when it actually responded. I kneeled down and picked up a curious-looking brown rock. This was no ordinary rock, and I knew instantly when I saw the arises on the dorsal side and the fine retouch along the edge that I was holding a piece of ancient, unwritten history. It spanned the length of my palm and I intook a large, sharp breath of air. Too sharp. It hurt. . . .

Allen entered the point as a "lithic isolate off centerline" and Toby asked me to carry it back to camp. It was already past seven o'clock, so we quickly started moving again. Inside my pocket was the remnants of the Dune People, pulsating with a warmth and energy that put a tingling in my toes and stood the little hairs on my arms up on their ends. . . .

"You know we can't collect this," Bill said. "You need to go put it back." . . .

"It's just a rock," he said. "There are thousands of blades in this world. I don't know why people collect anything anymore. Besides, our permit says no collection and I can't break the law." He was firm. Viciously, hideously firm.

"No," Toby said, shaking his head. "We take it back tomorrow to where we found it. We did not find it here; we can't leave it here."

I breathed a sigh of relief, and when Bill handed me the artefact, I gripped it tightly with newfound care and respect, as if to say to it, "I will not leave you." As we drove back to camp I kept it in the pocket of my coat, safe in a womb of black polarfleece. I stroked it gently with my thumb, feeling its soft texture and gentle curve, sharp edges.

It is still there. I will sleep with it near me. Why does she cling to this

original artifacts have an inherent aura is an understanding of material culture as having an essential, unchangeable core that distinguishes originals from copies. What is ignored is the role of archaeology in determining which objects do or do not have aura, in this case Arnesen's learned ability to identify and value an ancient stone tool in a particular way corresponding to the conventions adopted by the project she was working for.

The experience of the aura and authenticity of an object can be cre-

little piece of rock? they wonder. It's just an artefact. Maybe it's that this is my first field season and I have not yet become jaded. They remember the times when artefacts were fascinating and new and spectacular. Soon it becomes the cause of endless, tedious paperwork and I will grow to hate it, they say.

But I can still stand here, clinging to my ideology, which mandates that every piece of humanity is important. Even the smallest flake. I would feel more comfortable with that blade in my possession, where it could be put on a giant metaphorical pedestal and truly appreciated, than if it were left for dead on the road. I cannot do that. There is a war between my conscience and my job.

Tomorrow, under the watchful eyes of my crew of people who know that I would love to keep it, I will bury this artefact. Perhaps a piece of me will be buried with it? . . .

In the afternoon we journeyed back to where I found the chert blade. . . . And there we left it. We buried that beautiful, ancient rock and walked away. I stared over my shoulder, longingly, tripping over my feet. How could I be expected to watch my steps when I was walking away from the most beautiful, amazing thing I have ever found? . . .

Every step back to the car was painful as the artefact screamed at me. I felt like Lot and his wife, who were told, according to the Bible, to leave the city without looking back. She did [look back], and all was lost. Even as we loaded into the car, I kept my eyes forward. "Don't fail me now. You can do it," I consoled myself. "It wants to be at its home in the sand."

I wanted a home in the sand for myself. A nice, cozy home where I could bury my head in pillows of pulverized rock and be with the remains of the Dune People.

Source: Arnesen 2001.

ated and (re-)negotiated by archaeologists and others. In effect, the aura of one and the same artifact can be present or absent at different times or in different places. As the eminent geographer David Lowenthal (1985: 240) notes, the felt past is, more than anything else, "a function of atmosphere as well as locale." Concerning the practice of archaeological fieldwork, Thomas Yarrow (2003: 68) argues accordingly that the objectivity and genuineness of archaeological artifacts is created through social circumstances, such as the outcome of discussions among the archaeologists on site and the subsequent perception that the sites have been excavated "properly" and "professionally," i.e., corresponding to current conventions.

The emphasis on atmosphere, locale, perception, and convention in experiencing the authentic past resembles the circumstances within which medically prescribed placebos can be highly effective treatments against various kinds of diseases and illnesses. Indeed, similar placebo effects can be at work regarding cultural experiences. In tourism research, it is well known that authenticity can be subtly staged for visitors, in other words, artificially created. For instance, the back regions of shops, restaurants, or sightseeing attractions can be deliberately set up to look more intimate and authentic than their fronts, thus confirming the tourists' expectations and manipulating their desire for authentic experiences (MacCannell 1973). "Rare" natural sights and wildernesses require considerable artificial creation and maintenance, too (see, e.g., Krieger 1973; Hennig 1999: 169–72). Disney theme parks excel generally in creating authentic experiences through complete artifice, and Euro Disneyland's English pub Toad Hall in France is arguably far more authentic than many pubs in England (Shanks 1995: 19; see also chapter 8). A similar point could undoubtedly be made in relation to archaeological heritage attractions and exhibitions. For example, as part of a major 2000 exhibition titled "Seven Hills— Pictures and Signs from the 21st Century" and held in Berlin, the German artist Klaus Heid displayed artifacts and historical interpretations about the ancient Khuza culture, which he invented himself (Heid 1995– 2000). When the press unveiled his work as fake and called it a scandalous lie, he pointed to his "suggestofictitious" method and maintained, as he had said all along, that the Khuza culture gives us decisive clues as to who we are and where we are coming from. In other words, we are those for whom authentic artifacts are not the reason but the consequence of a particular appreciation of ancient cultures.

It can easily be observed that visitors to archaeological sites or museums experience authenticity and aura in front of ancient originals to exactly the same extent as they do in front of very good reproductions or copies—as long as they do not know them to be reproductions or copies. A case in point is the prehistoric menhir that in 1987 was discovered during build-

Thesis 9:
Authenticity depends on the context of the observer.

ing work in Tübingen-Weilheim in Germany (see chapter 6). Two years later, a replica was erected near the spot where the find had been made (figure 7.1 top). The original stone had by then been transported to the State Museum of Württemberg in Stuttgart. Based on this knowledge, there was little doubt among the local population of Weilheim that whereas the stone in their village was a replica, the stone on display in the museum was the original (figure 7.1 bottom). There was no public information telling them otherwise. In fact, however, the museum had produced a second replica for display and left the original in its cellars. It was much too heavy to be placed elsewhere. People's understandings of the two stones' materialities turned out to be entirely determined by the fact that they could touch and knock on the hollow-sounding object in their village, whereas this was not customary behavior in the museum.

Intriguingly, some objects retain a very strong aura even when it is openly stated that the actual material of which they consist is more recent. A useful example is the Vasa, an enormous Swedish warship that sank shortly after leaving the Stockholm shipyard on August 10, 1628. After having been salvaged in 1961, it was found that the "wood," especially those surfaces directly exposed to the water, had decomposed to such an extent that up to eight kilograms of water were contained in one kilogram of the original dry wood. During a laborious preservation treatment lasting seventeen years, this water was gradually replaced by polyethylenglycol (PEG). Although the ship also contains a lot less decomposed wood elsewhere, when we admire the ship in the Vasa Museum, we are actually looking mostly at modern PEG. Some of the associated, separate artifacts now consist even practically entirely of PEG. Despite this, the ship and its artifacts retain a powerful presence as rescued and preserved originals from the seventeenth century. Ironically, it is precisely the treated surfaces that appear to evoke the presence of the past, although those parts of the ship that were missing and had to be replaced with modern wood actually resemble the material substance of the original much better than the rest.

It is clear from examples like this that we need to rethink the way we understand the materiality of ancient objects.

Authentic Copies

An object is not old or authentic as such, but it is de facto being "made" old and authentic through particular, contextual conditions and processes

(a)

(b)

Figure 7.1 (a) Replica of a menhir erected near the site of discovery in Tübingen-Weilheim, Baden-Württemberg, Germany, 1991; (b) the genuine artifact? Replica of the same menhir in the Württembergisches Landesmuseum (State Museum of Württemberg), Stuttgart, 1992. Photographs by Cornelius Holtorf, 1991/1992.

taking place in the present (see Holtorf 2002). In a way, archaeological research projects and exhibitions are not consequences of existing ancient artifacts, but ancient artifacts are consequences of existing archaeological research projects or exhibitions. As Shanks (1995: 20) writes, "An object's value is decided in moving from past to present through the work of desire." This desire may be the anticipation of the archaeologist to find a (particular kind of) artifact, or it may be the keenness of the visitor to marvel at ancient treasures, study traces of our forebears, or simply enjoy the experience of pastness during a direct encounter with something old. Occasionally, as with the museum replica of the menhir, this desire may be so strong that the object's value effectively moves from present to past. In Sweden, two earth-and-stone constructions built according to local tradition by children, one in the 1940s and the other in 1974, had over the course of only a few decades become registered ancient monuments that even featured official information boards explaining their ancient context. Although the tradition of building such sites may indeed have been ancient, the sites themselves were not as old as modern desire would have it (Myrberg 2004).

I do not mention these examples in order to argue in favor of fooling people with replicas and forgeries, although this is easy to accomplish even when it is possible to touch the objects (see Whittaker and Stafford 1999). More to the point is Umberto Eco's (1990: 181) insight that a forgery is such only for an external observer who knows the true properties of an object: "Something is not a fake because of its internal properties, but by virtue of a claim of identity. Thus forgeries are first of all a pragmatic problem."

Eco goes on to discuss criteria for acknowledging originals and exposing fakes. He concludes that many of the key concepts involved, for example, truth and falsity, authenticity and forgery, are circularly defined by each other and do not allow for a clear-cut set of rules on which to base our decisions (Eco 1990: 197–201). Similarly, the German sociologist Gerhard Schulze argues in his influential book *Die Erlebnis-Gesellschaft* (1993: 442–43) that in our society subjectively believed properties of things matter more than their objective properties. Customers are increasingly interested in buying particular experiences, rather than services and tools for specific practical needs. Consumers' satisfaction is thus dependent on what they believe themselves to have bought, not what they actually bought. This insight can also be applied to the way (ancient) material culture is valued in our society. It often seems as if the art objects and antiquities we own, view, or find are first and foremost intended to authenticate us, i.e., our own taste and status, rather than vice versa (see Lowenthal 1992: 189; Schulze 1993: 142–50).

A few more case studies demonstrate the complexity of these matters in practice. In the United States a concrete replica of a fully reconstructed Stonehenge III was build by Sam Hill in Maryhill, Washington, to commemorate thirteen young men who had lost their lives during World War I. Hill found this architectural reference appropriate for he was mistakenly informed that the original Stonehenge had been used as a sacrificial site. Other errors he made include the fact that his monument contains less than half of the correct number of bluestone replicas, its Heel Stone is in the wrong place, and the astronomers who advised the builder miscalculated where the midsummer sun would emerge at the horizon. As a result, on midsummer the various elements do not properly come together as they should. Nevertheless pagan worshippers have been more than happy to hold their authentic celebrations there (Kaiser 1998). As some form of compensation, it has been pointed out that at least in one respect the replica is superior to and more authentic than the original: "Sunset visitors can still drive doughnuts in front of the monolith—the way the Druids would have wanted it" (www.roadsideamerica.com/tour/nw4.html, accessed October 4, 2004).

In 1999 a 1:1 replica of Goethe's Garden House in the German city of Weimar was built very close to the original (see Krämer 1999; Vernissage 1999). It was made to look exactly identical to the original, both inside and outside. Using professional workmanship and a few chemical tricks, the new house and furniture were given some wear and tear so as to age more than two hundred years in a matter of days. Aside from their precise location and the possible results of detailed analyses of the materials involved, the differences between the two houses were initially apparent mainly through the way they were presented. The false house neither had a garden nor guards. Because it is not an original, visitors were allowed in freely, and they could (initially) touch everything. This practice was however discontinued when the copy started to look older than the original because of its heavier traffic of visitors. Whether or not the two houses were actually perceived differently by visitors, any contemporary experience of either house had, in any case, very little to do with how Goethe experienced his own house. When he first moved here in 1776, it was a couple of centuries old, unaffected by the impact of twentieth century bombs and restoration, and not in any way associated with Goethe. As Lowenthal (1992: 185–86) puts it, visitors of museums and historical sites or performances

> are ineluctably of their own time. What they make of what they see is similarly shaped by events and habits that postdate the relics on view. ... Time's erosions and accretions are bound to alter both physical substances and modes of perception. Those who profess to see things with the eyes or mind of the past are misled or enmeshed in fakery.

When commercial interests get involved the stakes are higher, and the methods get craftier. Tim Schadla-Hall was once fortunate enough to meet a couple in Sussex in the early 1960s, who explained that they had once met Sir Mortimer Wheeler on Chesil Beach. Wheeler had some workmen with him who were filling sacks with the rounded beach pebbles of which Chesil Beach (now protected as a World Heritage Site) is largely composed. They explained that the purpose of this activity only became clear subsequently when they visited the excavations at Maiden Castle, the famous Iron Age hill fort in southern England and saw a pile of Iron Age sling stones on sale to raise money for the excavation. It is almost certain that any stone slingshot recovered archaeologically by Wheeler during the excavations at Maiden Castle originated from Chesil Beach, where there still is a good supply. The only discernible difference between slingshots recovered from Chesil Beach in the 1930s and those recovered in the Iron Age is that the latter were selected and presumably transported by prehistoric people; the raw material was the same. As the material that was apparently sold had not been altered, as far as one can tell, and came from the same natural source as the material that was found in situ, it is difficult to see that this reported incident did any harm to the purchasers. They presumably were under the impression that they had in their possession a perfectly genuine Iron Age sling stone. Quite possibly, however, visitors would still have been interested in the sling stones even if Wheeler had mentioned that his own workmen had collected them. As the case of Goethe's Garden House showed, too, artifacts that are openly declared to be modern reproductions do not necessarily attract less public interest than originals (see also Lowenthal 1985: 290–91; 355–56; Whittaker and Stafford 1999: 208–209).

Revealing, also, is the modern cult around Harley-Davidson motorcycles (Håkan Karlsson personal communication). These motorcycles are still being built using technical solutions of the 1940s and 1950s. The authentic sound and vibrations from the big V-Twin motor are important parts of the cult, but they are dependent on old technical solutions: as a result everything shakes lose quickly, requiring the skills of the "lone rider" who can repair his "horse." Today, a small industry supplies proud Harley-Davidson owners with reproduced spare parts that guarantee the authenticity of both bike and rider. In effect, a modern owner of an ancient Harley-Davidson can ride a rebuilt and customized motorbike that may consist of more authentic parts than it did when it arrived new from the factory. Ironically, the number of replica parts produced in the present probably exceeds by far the number of the original parts ever produced in the past.

In the interest of authenticity, it may even be desirable to do away with original remains altogether. The futurologist Robert Jungk (2000: 7) once expressed the idea that ruins from the past, such as desecrated temples, rifled burial chambers, razed castles, and sacked palaces, in fact falsify history. We turn to them reverently to admire when we ought to recoil from them in horror, weeping over the violence, unscrupulousness, and crime that they signify.

If original remains tend to falsify the past, reproductions and reconstructions can be more faithful and authentic than what once actually existed. Antiquities must to some extent conform to modern assumptions of the past in order to be credible as (pre-)historical witnesses. If they fail to match our expectations, their genuine origin may be doubted (cf. Rehork 1987). In that way, the recreated past can indeed be superior to the original remains, even in its perceived authenticity, and hence assume the place of those remains (Lowenthal 1985: 354). This suggests, as the following chapter argues, that the experience of pastness is very much defined by values of each present rather than by what is actually still there from the past.

Edgar Rice Burroughs' popular novels about the imaginary past world of Pellucidar located inside the hollow earth did not become successful because their stories could actually have occurred in "reality" and surviving past races and species could actually be found inside the Earth. As Phillip Burger suggests in his afterword (Burroughs 2000), it was the novels' "patina of truth" that appealed widely, i.e., the scientific flair and realism they contained. They were not carried by prehistory, but by *prehistoricness*. By the same token, the centers of the Polish cities of Warsaw and Gdansk, although they were fully reconstructed after World War II, are distinctively medieval today (see Lowenthal 1985: 290–91). The rebuilding respected neither the original function nor all of the remaining original substance and, instead, put the main emphases on aesthetics and modern functionality. Yet more than half a century after the war, not only the tourists but also the new generation of Gdansk inhabitants identify with the "old" center. The Polish art historian Konstanty Kalinowski (1993) concludes from this that people do not always distinguish between original remains and reconstructed sham and treat their surroundings as changeable stage settings. The success of the rebuilt Polish town centers, Kalinowski fears, suggests to people that since destroyed originals can be reproduced, the protection of original historical substance is hardly necessary. Indeed, the 1920s reinforced-concrete replica of the Parthenon in Nashville, Tennessee, is said to be so authentic "that the Greeks would have to study the correct details in Nashville in order to rebuild the original" (Lowenthal 1985: 291). I return to this important issue of conservation and renewability in the next chapter.

The same principles apply to portable artifacts. For example, the rapidly expanding British high-street chain *Past Times* advertises "authentic replicas" in its catalog, while Greek tourist shops praise their handmade "original copies" (figure 7.2). The Danish company Museums Kopi Smykker offers "authentic copies" of ancient jewelry that, according to an advertisement from 1999, "is cast and handcrafted to such a level of perfection that the items look just as if they had been made yesterday in an ancient smithy." All copies from Museums Kopi Smykker are marked with a registered hallmark and may not be copied or imitated themselves. The objects are therefore both originals and copies; they are new and ancient at the same time. The German replica producer Markus Neidhardt adopts a similar marketing strategy. His catalog resembles in both content and layout a museum catalog (www.replik.de, accessed April 15, 2003). The jewelry advertised is praised as "authentic" in two seemingly

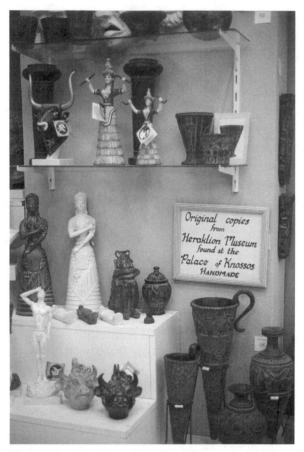

Figure 7.2 "Original copies from Heraklion Museum found at the Palace of Knossos Handmade." Shop window in Agios Nikolaos on the Greek island of Crete (cf. Loukatos 1978). Photograph by Cornelius Holtorf, 1996.

contradictory ways: the pieces are not only strictly based on "archaeological finds of particular quality" but at the same time contain irregularities and mistakes originating from the handicraft replicating process in which the new originals are being manufactured. The traces of the modern replicating process themselves thus render the reproduction authentic.

Omero Bordo, "the last Etruscan," takes another route to authenticity. According to a German newspaper report (*Welt am Sonntag*, April 21, 2002), in 1975 Omero was sentenced to two and a half years in prison for faking Etruscan antiquities. He always rejected the accusations by insisting that, although inspired by antiquities, he never produced anything but originals. After years of experiments, Omero claims to have rediscovered the ancient techniques. Because these originals cannot be discerned from originals, "even through the most sophisticated tests," they all come with a signed certificate of origin and authenticity confirming that Omero made them (etruscopoli.it, accessed October 4, 2004). Today, he runs his own tourist attraction called Etruscopolis, complete with reconstructed tombs and Etruscan vases and bronzes, all of which he makes himself.

As all these examples demonstrate, Lowenthal (1992: 188) is right in stating that "an original is authentic simply by definition; a replica is made authentic by hard work."

The Politics of Authenticity

These examples show that the experience of age and authenticity and ultimately the aura of an artifact itself depend first and foremost on particular meaningful experiences of that artifact by an observer in the present. The experience of age relies on an aesthetic that is established through elements such as design, manufacturing technique, traces of wear/use, patina, incompleteness, and so forth. Ultimately, it is the assumption of antiquity that matters, not its veracity (Lowenthal 1985: 242). The heritage experts John Tunbridge and Greg Ashworth (1996: 10–11) argue similarly:

> Authenticity in the heritage model derives from the experience of the consumer and specifically from the extent that the product satisfies whatever expectations the consumer has of the past. . . . Heritage is therefore what and where we say it is: it is the "we" in these contexts, not the object itself, that determines the authenticity.

What do I conclude from all this? I argue in this chapter that culturally more important than the actual age of a site or artifact is its perceived pastness, i.e., the way it allows the past to be experienced. Like age, aura and authenticity are not neutral "natural" properties of artifacts or sites but are context dependent. Their experience is constructed in and by particular present contexts. The material basis of archaeological heritage is thus not stable and permanent but subject to constant renegotiations and

Figure 7.3 Absolut Original (1988). Was this the original bottle? Conveying an authentic sense of pastness. From the official image description: "It was in 1987 when Richard Lewis [of TBWA Chiat/Day, Absolut's advertising agency] took his family to Iraq to participate in an archaeological dig, that they found a marble relic from 2500 b.c. The relic thus became the inspiration for Tom McManus' and Dave Warren's Absolut Original." Reproduced by permission of V&S Vin & Sprit AB. Absolut Country of Sweden Vodka & Logo, Absolut, Absolut bottle design and Absolut calligraphy are trademarks owned by V&S Vin & Spirit AB © 2002 by V&S Vin & Spirit AB.

even manipulations (cf. Lowenthal 1985; 1992; 1994; Bruner 1994). In other words, the materiality of a thing is not its essential property but the result of relationships of people and things: it is potentially multiple and has a history (cf. Shanks 1998; Thomas 1996: 70–82).

If one of the tasks of archaeology consists of supplying our communities with authentic experiences of the archaeological past, archaeologists must learn and make use of the particular skills it takes to do this, rather than simply amass artifacts and write texts about them. It will be helpful to do further research in order to understand better how materiality, authenticity, age-value, and pastness are created and perceived: their aesthetic properties, their social roles and functions, the means of their creation, and the cultural patterns of their appreciation. Such a notion of material substance, the past, age, and authenticity challenges some basic tenets of heritage management, in particular that of the past and its material remains as nonrenewable resources. To that issue I turn next.

THE PAST AS A RENEWABLE RESOURCE

"This home is very historical," they say. "But it was built only last year."

—David Lowenthal (1994: 63, referring to F. W. Mote 1973)

I have argued that authenticity and pastness are constructed in each present. They are not properties inherent in any material form. This leads to the conclusion that each present constructs not only the past in its own terms but even the age and authenticity of the material remains of that past. Are the past and its remains, then, really nonrenewable resources as is often stated?

Is the Past Endangered?

It has become a cliché to lament the loss of ancient sites and objects in the modern Western world in much the same way as we do the continuous reduction of the tropical rainforests and the gradual decline of remaining oil reserves (cf. Lomborg 2001). Timothy Darvill argues accordingly that "the archaeological resource is finite in the sense that only so many examples of any defined class of monument were ever created. . . . The archaeological resource is non-renewable in that . . . once a monument or site is lost it cannot be recreated" (1993: 6).

Similarly to the decrease of important natural resources, it has been reckoned that this generation has destroyed more of prehistory than was previously known to exist (Lowenthal 1985: 396). As a consequence, rescue archaeology and the preservation of ancient sites have become the order of the day. The UNESCO World Heritage Centre, for example, writes about its task:

With 754 cultural and natural sites already protected worldwide, the World Heritage Committee is working to make sure that future generations can inherit the treasures of the past. And yet, most sites face a variety of threats, particularly in today's environment. The preservation of this common heritage concerns us all. (www.unesco.org/whc/nwhc/pages/sites/s_worldx.htm, accessed October 4, 2004)

But all of this could be beside the point. I argue in this chapter that we are not at any risk of running out of archaeological sites and monuments and that future generations of people will never be without "treasures of the past." The cultural heritage does not disappear steadily in the same way the ozone layer or the rainforest do, for two reasons.

First, in absolute terms we are arguably not actually losing but gaining sites. No other societies have surrounded themselves with as many archaeological sites and objects that can be experienced in the landscape or as part of collections as our modern Western societies. Typical for the Western world is not the loss of archaeological sites and objects but their rescue and subsequent accumulation in museums, archives, or the landscape. Even archaeologists themselves will agree that the rapidly growing numbers of archaeological sites and objects creates considerable challenges for responsible heritage management and the archiving of finds, making it difficult to keep up with the overall task of "writing history" (Tilley 1989b). In relation to the huge accumulation of data from extensive rescue work, we are arguably the victims of our own success. If there is any problem concerning the preservation of archaeological sites and objects in the modern Western world, it could therefore be that we are overwhelmed by the sheer number of them. This problem has been building up for some time and exists equally in the United States and in Europe (see Thomas 1991; Robbins 2001). In 1995, England alone (not the United Kingdom as a whole) had more than 657,000 registered archaeological sites, an increase of 117 percent since 1983, and its archaeological site and monument records were expected to contain over one million entries by the end of the millennium. Between 1983 and 1995, on average nearly one hundred entries were added to the records daily, while only one recorded site per day has been lost since 1945 (according to Darvill and Fulton 1998: 4–7). The trend is therefore not that we will one day have no archaeological sites and finds left, but that in the future more and more of our lifeworld will be recorded and stored as some sort of historical object worthy of appreciation and preservation.

Second, far more important than counting the number of preserved or destroyed sites or objects is ensuring that the benefits the cultural heritage offers to people remain available to future generations (for similar arguments concerning natural resources, cf. Krieger 1973; Lomborg 2001: 119). Before lamenting loudly any losses, it is therefore pertinent to ask what we need the cultural heritage for. Different purposes may be fulfilled by different kinds of sites, and even though we are not in danger of running out of ancient sites completely, we may be in danger of running out of particularly valuable sites. This possibility clearly warrants further study. Here, I show, however, that both archaeologists' and nonarchaeologists' appreciations of ancient sites are not directly related to any specific amount of preservation and may not require the preservation of many original sites at all.

One of the benefits of cultural heritage is often said to be the possibility of appreciating the historical roots of our present, thereby cultivating a critical historical consciousness (e.g., Wienberg 1999: 191). But if anything, the reverse is true: cultural heritage is not the origin but the manifestation of a historical consciousness and various specific appreciations of the past. As a cultural construct the past does not necessarily rely on great numbers of original archaeological sites or objects. Their significance for our understandings of the past depends largely on the wider sociocultural contexts within which they are given value, meaning, and legal protection (see Leone and Potter 1992). Every generation constructs its own range of ancient sites and objects, which function as metaphors that evoke the past. Certain pasts may not even directly relate to physical remains of the past at all (see Layton 1994).

Over the centuries, many novel pasts replaced others. The sociologist George Herbert Mead states, "Every generation rewrites its history—and its history is the only history it has of the world" (1929: 240). With every new past, new archaeological and historical sites and objects are created or become significant in relation to this past. Others become redundant and eventually disappear. This may be sad, but only in the way that the autumn is sad (Vayne 2003: 15). As the eminent economist Alan Peacock phrases it, "we should not assume that the 'non-reproducible' is necessarily 'irreplaceable'" (1978: 3).

Thesis 10:

The past is being remade in every present and is thus a renewable resource.

As far as our own present society is concerned, one can gain the impression that "archaeological material is not protected because it is valued, but rather it is valued because it is protected" (Carman 1996: 115). This view is similar to physicist Martin Krieger's (1973) argument in an infamous *Science* paper regarding the natural environment. He claims that the way Americans experience nature, including "rare environments," is conditioned by their society and the result of conscious choices about what is desired, followed by investments and advertising to create these desired experiences. The interventions that create these rare environments in the first place can also create plentiful substitutions.

To complicate matters further, at any one time there are various parallel pasts with their own set of meaningful archaeological sites and objects. John Tunbridge and Greg Ashworth argue in respect to modern society

> there is an almost infinite variety of possible heritages, each shaped for the requirements of specific consumer groups. . . . An obvious implication that needs constant reiterating is that the nature of the heritage product is determined . . . by the requirements of the consumer not the existence of the resources. (1996: 8, 9)

What constitutes an ancient site or object for some may not necessarily do so for others, who may consider it fake, misinterpreted, or unscientific. Preservationists, druids, New Age followers, archaeoastronomers, ley hunters, political parties, and others each reinvent the past in their own terms and with reference to their own selection of especially significant ancient sites and artifacts, which can be very different from those of academic archaeology. In each case the selection of objects follows from the perspective taken and not vice versa.

Another kind of social benefit of the cultural heritage is that they give people the possibility of permanently rescuing them. In some cases, documenting and saving remains of the past has become more important than what is actually documented and saved (see chapter 4). Luckily, we will not run out of savable ancient sites any time soon, and archaeology can therefore remain significant as a practice of documentation, preservation, and rescue for a long time to come. Wildlife conservation plays a similar role, and it is occasionally informative to connect the two discourses of archaeological and natural conservation. Charles Bergman, a professor of

English specializing in environmental writing, observed recently that the cultural significance of wild animals is in part linked to the category "endangered": "We like animals because they are endangered. . . . We don't want animals do go extinct. Nor do we want them abundant. We want them endangered. . . . Endangerment signifies a category in which animals are known by their perpetual disappearing" (2002).

Their marginal state of existence gives these animals one of their characteristic values—and it gives humans the opportunity to contribute to their perpetual rescue. What matters a lot in nature conservation, as in much of cultural-heritage management, is the metaphorical significance of what lies beyond our everyday surroundings. Insofar as they have a strange appearance, remote origins, and their numbers are threatened, both animals and artifacts can become exotic rarities. People enjoy helping them to survive as such but would not want them to become too common.

Other benefits of cultural heritage include pragmatic effects (they generate income and create jobs) and political functions (they help build collective identities and support ideologies). Copies and reconstructions need to be made and managed too, though. And they too can be used for social and political engineering, signifying a range of valued metaphors. All the benefits mentioned so far, therefore, do not straightforwardly depend on the extensive preservation of a given, large assemblage of cultural heritage.

But what about the benefits of preserving archaeological sites and objects for the benefit for future generations of archaeologists who will be able to employ improved methods and, therefore, learn a lot more about the past? Arguably, large numbers of preserved archaeological sites are not as essential for scientific research as is often stated. This is not because I trust that we can record them "in full" at the time of their destruction or because I believe a small sample of sites would in any case be representative. Rather, I am inclined to think that the success of archaeology is determined by how satisfactorily the norms of its craft, or discourse, are exercised in practice and not by some objective measure of how close we have come to an understanding of the "real" past (cf. Shanks and McGuire 1996). In other words, archaeologists will be happy to do their fieldwork and analyze site and monument records with ever-new questions and methods, to write smart academic books and papers, and to teach their students, no matter how many archaeological sites are left at their disposal. Indeed, it may even stimulate research and interpretation if the amount of data available is limited rather than overwhelming. At least in informal discussions this is sometimes given as the reason for the greater willingness of prehistorians to concern themselves with interpretation and theory than, for example, classical or historical archaeologists.

At any rate, what benefits in the present are we prepared to sacrifice for the good of future generations? On what basis can anybody deny present communities the right to use their heritage however they see fit? It is quite impossible to know and is, perhaps, a peculiar kind of arrogance to assume that future generations will be grateful to us for preserving vast amounts of ancient material culture (Moore 1997: 31). It is also politically, economically, and ethically debatable whether it is right, despite many urgent present-day needs and various legitimate interests in consuming ancient sites, to spend tight public resources on future generations' presumed interests (cf. Merriman 2002). Their preferences will by definition always remain unknown since the future can never be present. But if one wants to risk any prediction at all, they are likely to be materially better off than we are today and thus economically less deserving than we are ourselves, Alan Peacock (1978: 7) has asserted. Moreover, it may arguably be counterproductive to preserve too much for future generations since they may perceive as less valuable what is less rare and thus be less appreciative and careful than they would otherwise have been, effectively rendering our conservation efforts meaningless (Krieger 1973: 453).

Experiencing the Past

Michael Shanks (1995) has claimed that archaeology, like heritage, is largely a set of experiences. Simulated environments can provide us with fabricated, but nevertheless real, experiences of both the "authentic" past and archaeology (see chapter 7). Their realism is not that of a lost, real past but of real sensual impressions and emotions in the present, which engage visitors and engender meaningful feelings (see Bagnall 1996; Hjemdahl 2002). Among the most powerful "archaeological" events, sites, and objects evoking the past in our present without being able to withstand a scientific dating test are

- Models and dioramas in exhibitions

- Virtual reconstructions in computer games (cf. Watrall 2002)

135

- Facsimile reprints of ancient texts and replicas of artifacts, such as those for sale in tourist shops and museums (figure 7.2)

- Art installations in the tradition of the *Spurensicherung* (see figures 4.1, 4.2, and 4.4)

- Souvenirs, retro-chic, and other items of popular culture that draw on designs evoking the past (figures 7.3 and 8.1; cf. Loukatos 1978)

- Living history, historic plays, and reenactments of past events, either live or on film (cf. Samuel 1994: part II; Gustafsson 2002)

- Restored or reconstructed archaeological heritage sites such as Stonehenge and the fast growing number of archaeological open-air museums (figures 5.2, 6.1, 6.2, and 7.1; cf. Petersson 2003)

- Artificial ruins, Egyptian and Greek temples in landscape parks and zoological gardens from the eighteenth and nineteenth centuries (figure 9.2)

- Reconstructed buildings and entire town districts, as in the Polish cities of Warsaw and Gdansk (see chapter 7)

- Reenacted traditions such as the annual initiation ceremony of the Welsh *Gorsedd of Bards* performed in modern stone circles

- Rebred, formerly extinct animal species such as the Przewalski horse

- Neo-Gothic, neoclassical, and certain elements of contemporary postmodern architecture, mostly in America (e.g., in Las Vegas, see front cover; cf. Lowenthal 1985: 309–19, 382–83; Dyson 2001)

Some of these elements also occur both in Disneyland and in the themed hotel-casino-shopping malls of Las Vegas. The range of Disney products in particular is interesting here since they are not only very popular but also very experience-oriented. Moreover, Disney products provide

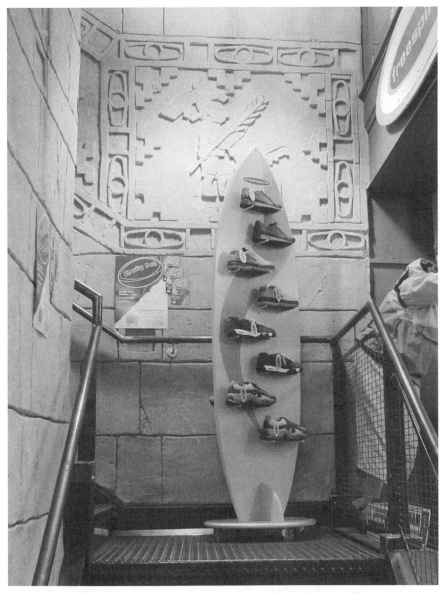

Figure 8.1 Maya art in central Cambridge, United Kingdom. Staircase in the sportshop Freespirit. Photograph by Cornelius Holtorf, 2001.

potent imagery about the past (cf. Fjellman 1992: 59–63; Silverman 2002). The American public historian Mike Wallace (1985: 33) speculates in an often-cited essay that Walt Disney through his theme parks may have taught people more history, in a more memorable way, than they ever learned in school. Behind the success of Disney are a number of more general principles that have now come to dominate more and more sectors of society. The British sociologist Alan Bryman (1999) distinguishes four such increasingly influential principles.

1. *Theming*: the use of imagery to which people can easily relate and which immerses them in a world different from the normal routines and restrictions of everyday life. Such metaphorical elsewhereness is not only exciting in itself but also carries the implication that there are different rules to observe and different responsibilities to attend to (see Hopkins 1990; Köck 1990). Theming is increasingly important for shopping areas, restaurants, hotels, golf courses, and even entire city centers, not just in Las Vegas (see Gottdiener 1997; Beardsworth and Bryman 1999). Board games and toys are often themed too (see, e.g., figure 3.3). Even entire countries are theming themselves in their attempts to attract tourists, transforming modern travel from an encounter with other cultures into an experience of attractive metaphors.

2. *Dedifferentiation of consumption*: forms of consumption associated with different institutional spheres that become interlocked with each other and are increasingly difficult to distinguish. For example, as Disneyland and Las Vegas illustrate, the distinction between hotel–shop–amusement park–theme park is disappearing. Theme parks have hotels and house shops, casinos incorporate hotels and museums, and shops are increasingly themed and can provide various kinds of amusements, slowly transforming them into tourist attractions in themselves (see Hopkins 1990). Traditional tourist attractions like museums and heritage sites, on the other hand, rely increasingly on revenues generated by their shops.

3. *Merchandising*: promotion of goods connected with copyrighted images and logos. While Disney throughout his busi-

ness empire has led the way in marketing logos and characters by carefully controlling all rights to them, similar merchandising techniques have now spread to various restaurant chains (such as the Hard Rock Cafe) and even to universities. I still occasionally get special offers for branded products from the University of Reading where I was a visiting student fourteen years ago.

4. *Emotional labor*: employers seeking to control their workers' emotions. The insistence that workers have to exhibit cheerfulness and friendly smiles towards customers at all times is as common in Disneyland as it is in McDonald's restaurants and a range of other (American) shops.

As a result of these four principles at work, consumption is increasingly linked to signification, lifestyle, and identity (Gottdiener 1997: 153–54). The powerful associations and positive connotations of archaeology as the adventure of investigating the human past may be able to account for its ubiquity not only in Disneyland's Frontierland and Adventureland, but also in other Disneyfied areas of contemporary society like museums, shops, and hotels. Disneyland's own most archaeological attraction is the exhilarating Indiana Jones Adventure ride based on elements of the movie *Indiana Jones and the Temple of Doom*.

Disneyfied history is qualitatively different from school history: it improves the past and represents what history should (!) have been like; it celebrates America, technological progress, and nostalgic memory; it hides wars, political and social conflicts, and human misery (cf. Wallace 1985; Fjellman 1992: chapter 4). Arguably, Disney history is false in as much as it is highly selective and simplistic rather than balanced and suitably complex; it is celebratory rather than critical; and it is profit oriented rather than educational. It is true that in final analysis, Disney "magic" serves to hide the commercial interests of a huge and very profitable business. It is therefore easy to dismiss Disney theme parks and Disneyfied attractions elsewhere as the capitalist American way of commodifying our lives and manipulating our knowledge of both the past and the present.

It has been argued that such sites fool people, not merely by giving them the impression of something that is not what it seems, but mainly by perfecting a fantasy world of fakes, which is more real than reality ("hyperreal") and manipulates our perceptions, desires, and preferences (cf. Eco 1986; Fjellman 1992; Sanes 1996–2000a, 1996–2000b). This view, however, does not take the actual human experiences seriously enough. For, whatever purpose theming may serve, it still provides experiences that relate very closely to people's desires and identities. Disney heritage is clearly fabricated, but it has the virtue that a large part of the public loves it. This is significant, for theming has to be appreciated as a part of people's lived realities (cf. Bruner 1994; Lowenthal 1998). People are not tricked into believing in these worlds as alternatives to reality. Disney visitors are not fooled or misled. They are never made to believe that they are in any other period than the present. They always know that they can rely on the achievements of modernity: punctuality, physical safety, comfort, reliability, efficiency, cleanliness, hygiene, and the like are guaranteed.

Instead of insisting that themed environments provide illusions and hyperrealities, it is therefore more appropriate to see them as what sociologists Alan Beardsworth and Alan Bryman (1999) call "quasifications": they invite the visitor to experience them as if they were something other. Consumers can thus "'pretend' that they are embroiled in an experience that is outside the modern context, but which is in fact firmly and safely rooted in it" (Beardsworth and Bryman 1999: 248–49). According to this theory, theming works so well precisely because people know that they are in artificial environments saturated by metaphors: they enjoy marveling at evocative relics and convincing fabrications, especially when they recognize the experience created (or indeed parodied) and the general way in which it is done (see, e.g., McCombie 2001). People enjoy feeling that they are somewhere and sometime else than where and when they actually are.

The authenticity of that experience is sustained by an "emotional realism." Gaynor Bagnall (1996) argues that this emotional realism is underpinned by a desire for the experience to be genuine and based in fact. But many people neither seek historical veracity in themed environments nor mind its absence. They simply enjoy the sensual stimuli and experiences of imaginary spaces (cf. Hennig 1999; Hjemdahl 2002). Contrary to Bagnall's conclusions, a superficial appearance of factuality that is not actually believed can be sufficient to ensure emotional satisfaction.

People particularly enjoy experiences that bring them close to something they recognize from their collective imaginations and fantasies. Experiences of elsewhereness and otherness can thus be created by drawing on "virtual capital" that consumers derive from mass media such as cinema and especially television (see Hennig 1999: 94–101; Beardsworth and Bryman 1999: 252). This link has many manifestations, from stereotypical natural habitats as they are recreated, for example, in our zoos to the clichés presented in historical reconstructions and "living history" (see Gustafsson 2002: chapter 6). For example, one of the best-known, widely used images representing the Roman world in Western popular culture is that of the chained galley slave, even though this notion is demonstrably false and owes its popularity to the *Ben Hur* novel and films (James 2001). The dreamworld of Las Vegas works in a similar way. The sociologist Mark Gottdiener (1997: 106) observed from a single vantage point in the streets of Las Vegas as many as half a dozen widely shared cultural clichés that we can all relate to media such as the Discovery Channel and *National Geographic Magazine*: a giant Easter Island sculpted head, an immense lion, a huge medieval castle, and a giant Sphinx in front of a pyramid.

One way in which Disney creates its magic is by using precisely such stereotypes that people respond to without thinking: although no one has ever lived in the past, everybody knows what it looked like (cf. Mitchell 1998: 48). Fred Beckenstein, a senior Euro Disneyland manager, appropriately said in an interview, "we're not trying to design what really existed in 1900, we're trying to design what people think they remember about what existed" (cited in Dickson 1993: 34). This is also born out in the Disney movie *The Emperor's New Groove* (2000), which portrays the ancient Inca culture in Peru but draws in its imagery on a wide range of recognizably pre-Columbian or merely exotic, largely non-Inca and pre-Inca motifs (Silverman 2002). Taken to the extreme, what is fabricated in such a manner can thus seem more authentic and more valuable than what is actually ancient (see chapter 7).

From a purist point of view this may be very sad. But highly segmented markets require a focus on what is known to appeal in order for products to satisfy a large-enough proportion of consumers to be commercially viable (see Gottdiener 1997: chapter 7). In other words, for themed environments to work, their themes must be broadly consistent with the existing knowledge of the consumers. They will thus usually refer to tried-and-tested motifs of Western popular culture. That is why even the (in)famous, historically false, horned Viking helmet still has a certain legitimacy. As Alexandra Service argues in her study about the Vikings in twentieth-century Britain,

> To survive as something that people care about, as the inspiration and focus for re-enactment, novels, merchandising and theme restaurants, it is necessary to be memorable, to stand out from the crowd. There must be the potential for excitement, and for escape from humdrum reality. These are qualities which the Viking myth supplies in abundance. . . . So the Vikings' mixed reputation, horned helmets, red and white sails and all, live on. (1998b: 245–56)

Archaeological themes and icons such as those mentioned here renew the past in our time. In none of these examples is an explicit claim about true antiquity made, but they appear to be fully satisfactory in supplying many people with "authentic" experiences of the past and in satisfying

Figure 8.2   The large buffet restaurant "Pharaoh's Pheast" in the Luxor hotel/ casino is seemingly next to an ongoing excavation of Egyptian treasures where the archaeologists have just gone for lunch. Photograph by Cornelius Holtorf, 2001.

Archaeology at Las Vegas

An extreme example of the proliferation of themed environments is provided by the very successful and profitable hotel-casino-shops in Las Vegas. They metaphorically transport the customer into some other world, removed from daily life and its conventional responsibilities and controls, encouraging fantasy and, of course, spending which is really the point.

Caesars Palace opened in 1966 as the first Las Vegas resort to embody consistently an archaeological or historical theme. It signifies the popular myth of a decadent and opulent Rome associated with excess and indulgence as it is depicted in movies like *Ben Hur, Cleopatra,* or *Gladiator.* Arguably, Caesars Palace creates a museum for the mass audience, a museum free of admission fees, velvet ropes, and Plexiglas panels and (falsely) appearing to be free even of omnipresent security guards (McCombie 2001: 56; cf. Schulze 1993: 142–46). Its architecture and design bear the signs of historicity but lack the tedious labels. The hotel-casino is a carrier of culture without many of the explicit behavioral constraints and class implications found in many ordinary museums. It invites the visitor-customer even to relive the past. Jay Sarno, the original owner of Caesars Palace, reportedly claimed, "We wanted to create the feeling that everybody in the hotel was a Caesar" (hence, there is no apostrophe in Caesars; Malamud 1998: 13). Margaret Malamud recognized this as one version of the American Dream: "it offers each guest the chance to transcend economic constraints and social barriers; and the design, facilities, and amenities at the Palace promise glamour, the fulfillment of desire, wealth, and power" (1998: 14).

Almost the same might be same about the Luxor, a more recent Las Vegas resort. Here, too, an atmosphere of exotic luxuriousness is created to stimulate spending. Completed in 1993 in the shape of the world's largest pyramid and with a gigantic sphinx in front of it, the Luxor embraces the clichés of ancient Egypt, incorporating the pyramids, pharaohs, mummies, occult mysteries, fabulous wealth, and archaeological excavations. An "authentic" reproduction of Tutankhamun's tomb as it looked when Howard Carter opened it in 1922 lets the tourist slip into the role of the archaeologist discovering wonderful things (Malamud 2001: 35). The main lobbies of the building are filled with full-scale Egyptian architecture, and in each room walls, wardrobes, and bed linen are adorned with Egyptian-style murals and hieroglyphics. The local *What's On* journal even proclaims the Luxor to be "as much a museum as it is a hotel and casino." A fact sheet available in the hotel in 2001 stated not only that "all ornamentation and hieroglyphs are authentic reproductions of originals" but also that "our ten-story tall Sphinx is taller than the original Sphinx."

most of our educational, economic, aesthetic, and spiritual needs, among others. In a similar vein, Andreas Wetzel argues that archaeological ruins allow and invite visitors to construct an image of the past, but the "actual physical historicity is of absolutely no relevance" to their effective signifi-cance in the present (1988: 18). This implies neither that people are vic-tims of deliberate deceptions nor that they are superficial fools (cf. Cohen 1988). The ancient sites and objects archaeologists are normally dealing with do nothing other than renew the past in the present, too, often evok-ing potent metaphors. The value of archaeology in popular culture lies for the most part not in the specific results of its scholarship but in the degree to which it is linked to both the experience of pastness and to the grand themes of doing archaeology, as discussed in earlier chapters. In most cir-cumstances, accurate factual details as such are far less important than the bigger impressions conveyed and the overall imagery evoked.

Constructive Destruction

If the experience of the past can somehow take the place of the past itself, what does this imply for the conservation and preservation of ancient sites and artifacts as two traditional objectives of archaeology and heritage management?[1] They lose some of their currency and significance.

Ironically, modernism with its fetishization of the new and its desire to shape ever-new futures has also been characterized by a particular obsession with maintaining supposedly unchanging and objective monu-ments of the past (see Samuel 1994: 110; Fehr 1992: 54–56). All was to be modernized, apart from the remains of the past that needed to be pre-served as they were. But the dualism between preservation on the one hand and modernization or modern usefulness on the other is in fact mis-leading. Not only are many preserved archaeological sites highly efficient modern heritage sites, but the ongoing project of modernity has also been producing ever more documented archaeological sites and artifacts. If it were not for various destructive processes carried out in the name of mod-ernization, such as development, deep plowing, and war, many sites and

---

1. Although conservation (against human destruction) and preservation (for human consumption) are two distinct strategies, I will in the following not make this distinction and refer simply to preservation when I mean the opposite of destruction.

artifacts would have remained unacknowledged in the ground until they had completely decayed; in effect, they would not have existed for any archaeologist to study. Even within the philosophy of modernist archaeology, it is thus commonly accepted that sites may be destroyed, layer by layer, and artifacts removed from their depositional contexts, as long as all of this is being replaced by records, which are archived for the benefit of the archaeological discipline (see Lucas 2001a: 159). Although most of what is uncovered still ends up on the spoil heap, archaeologists find this practice perfectly acceptable and a price worth paying for being able to contribute to the grand project of modern archaeology.

Many archaeological sites and artifacts, however, are not normally allowed to be damaged in any way so that, it is said, they can keep their value. But the link between keeping certain values and preventing damage is not as straightforward as it may seem. Irrespective of the fact that the often-necessary preservation of artifacts or sites can be a destructive process in itself (cf. Wijesuriya 2001), fundamental conflicts between intended preservation and desired use may arise. As the history of Stonehenge as a tourist destination and meeting point illustrates (see chapter 5), certain genuine uses of a site may be considered adverse to its material preservation.

Yet, what some would call "destruction" might simply be a way of appreciating a site in a way others are not used to, possibly preserving its long-standing function and character. The South African archaeologist Sven Ouzman (2001) showed, for example, how southern African rock engravings were traditionally hammered, rubbed, cut, and flaked. Such practices allowed people to produce sounds, to touch numinous images and rocks, and to possess, even consume, pieces of potent places. To our own predominantly visual culture, it seems foreign, even regrettable, that such sites are being "diminished" in this way. But arguably, the engravings were always part of lifeways that are less sensually impaired and less fixated on material preservation than our own, and what was a loss to us was a gain to others. By the same token, the comprehensive restoration and rebuilding of ancient *stupas* (repositories for a relic of the Buddha) in Sri Lanka until the twentieth century may have been detrimental to the ancient buildings for some but was religiously highly significant for those involved (see Kemper 1991: chapter 5; Byrne 1995; Wijesuriya 2001).

Stopping such traditions means interfering with people's genuine

engagements with the past and the constructive creation of their own heritage. Preservation of the original substance would in effect create a different kind of site and a different kind of past, preventing these practices from taking place in the future. Destruction is thus not necessarily fundamentally different from preservation as both processes transform a site with certain aims. Even in the Western world, the conservation ethic constitutes a radical departure from a long-standing previous historical practice and may, by implication, at some point give way to an alternative set of values yet again (Byrne 1995: 275). Arguably, therefore, the principles of modern preservationism themselves provide an example for how the past can be renewed in a particular present.

It is important to recall that the life history of archaeological sites and artifacts includes all kinds of reinterpretation, reuse, vandalism, or other modification, whether in the name of destruction or preservation (see chapter 5). They are historically equally significant. The former editor of *Pagan News* magazine, Julian Vayne (2003: 14), expresses this point particularly well: "The history of the site is not 'damaged' when something is added or taken away. If I lose [or remove!] a button from my coat I have not 'damaged' its history. History is not a fixed thing but a continuum, a process."

How ancient sites or objects have been treated has always depended on the people involved and their particular preferences and agendas, much like today. Yet, since you cannot treat one and the same object in two different ways at the same time, it is impossible to please everybody. Hammering and flaking rock engravings cannot be combined with conserving the very same rock surfaces for the future. The anthropologist Mark Johnson (2001) discussed the same difficulty at the example of the World Heritage site of Hue in Vietnam. For UNESCO and possibly most visitors to Hue, the disappearance of buildings is seen as a problem when caused by humans, for example as a result of war. Yet when due to natural processes, decay is accepted and even valued as evidence of the natural locatedness, the romantic appeal, and the age-value of the site. But for a significant minority of visitors, U.S. Vietnam veterans, it is precisely the rubble of war that is most valued and appreciated at Hue. Using this example, Johnson argues that destruction is an inevitable part of every (re)construction, whether it is material or merely in our minds. You will always lose some things and gain others, although people may disagree strongly about the relative merits of the various possible actions taken. Johnson, thus, effectively relativizes destruction and calls for all claims to places, sites, and histories to acknowledge and account for the silences, suppressions, and vandalism that go together with their particular (re)constructions and representations (2001: 89).

A similar argument can be made regarding artifacts from ancient sites: in being physically altered or moved from one context to another, they lose some qualities and gain others. For example, as part of my personal collection of mementos and "things," I own a Punic arrowhead from Segesta on the southern Italian island of Sicily, which I received as a Christmas present in 1984. Clearly, this has got to be either a fake or an illicit antiquity. But that made little difference to me back then, as this little token of Carthaginian history was for years an item of great pride and metaphorical significance to me. I have always felt uneasy about owning a single mosaic stone from Ostia in Italy, which I took with me as a souvenir during a visit in 1987. What was I thinking, just one year before I began studying archaeology at university? Today, I am confident in admitting my satisfaction about actually possessing a piece of ancient Ostia, which is authentic because I picked it up myself (or were the managers of ancient Ostia more cunning than I thought?). Yes, if every visitor did the same, in a matter of years there would not be much left of sites like this. But in another sense it would also mean something quite wonderful, that a site continues to exist despite being delocalized, distributed in the minds and on the shelves of so many proud tourists around the world. I also own a tiny piece of the Berlin Wall which I collected back in January 1984, sneaking onto German Democratic Republic territory, which started one meter in front of the wall, and scraping with my fingernails. Since then, of course, the unique value and aura of this piece has been somewhat reduced by the historical events of 1989 and their material implications. The Berlin Wall has indeed become a fine example of a historical site of great sig-

> **Thesis 11:**
> In some cases much can be gained from effectively destroying an ancient site.

nificance that has now largely disappeared from its original location and whose parts have been dispersed around the world, each one making a considerable impact in its new context. I value all these pieces for the contexts within which they were recovered and collected, and the memories of my teens that I associate with them.

147

It is incorrect and somewhat naive to insist that looting makes ancient artifacts archaeologically as good as worthless by forever disassociating them from their precise original context within the given stratigraphy of the archaeological site from which they derive. This is a position that can only be understood within a very specific Western, academic way of thinking anyway. In fact, it is exactly these artifacts' precise, original context that makes them valuable as archaeological commodities and lets them become so significant as authentic artifacts in the new contexts of peoples' lives, to an extent that artifacts processed by an archaeological project and remaining in the public domain will struggle hard to even approach (see Byrne 1995: 276–77; Thoden van Velzen 1996; Ucko 2001; Stille 2002: chapter 3). Although illicit tomb robbing can harm all sorts of local, non-academic interests too, it is impossible to condemn all destructions of archaeological sites or objects categorically. In the cases just mentioned and related to the above-mentioned war-damaged Hue, southern African rock engravings, Sri Lankan *stupas*, and archaeological excavations generally, destructive activities can be seen as potentially having also (though not exclusively) important positive outcomes. A certain amount of destruction of archaeological resources is not only unavoidable but can indeed be desirable in order to accommodate fairly as many genuine claims to ancient sites and objects as possible (cf. Vayne 2003). As extraordinary as this conclusion may sound, it should not be seen as jeopardizing the archaeological project at large. Instead, it offers a new opportunity for overcoming some of the established oppositions between archaeologists and other heritage "users," such as collectors, developers, local communities, and other interested parties.

My main point in this chapter is that archaeological heritage management is and should be concerned with actively and responsibly renewing the past in our time. Instead of preserving too much in situ and endlessly accumulating finds and data for an unspecified future, it is more than appropriate to take seriously the challenge of providing experiences of the past that are actually best for our own society now (cf. Leone and Potter 1992). Archaeologists have the skills, experience, and responsibility to assist our society in constructing the pasts it desires—and deserves. As Tunbridge and Ashworth argue,

The production of heritage becomes a matter for deliberate goal-directed choice about what uses are made of the past for what contemporary purposes. . . . The recycling, renewal and recuperation of resources, increasingly important in the management of natural resources, can be paralleled in historic resources where objects including buildings can be moved, restored and even replicated. . . . The deliberate manipulation of created heritage can be a valuable instrument [in an efficient management of historic resources]. (1996: 9, 13)

When visiting a relic mound with a friend, anthropologist Steven Kemper (1991: 136) asked whether the place was ancient. "Yes," the friend replied. "It was restored just last year."

CHAPTER NINE
ARCHAEO-APPEAL

If it is the crime of popular culture that it has taken our dreams and packaged them and sold them back to us, it is also the achievement of popular culture that it has brought us more and more varied dreams than we could otherwise ever have known.

—Richard Maltby (1989: 14)

I started this book by stating that archaeology is a fascinating theme of our age and then claimed that it was significant to the world in which we live. In the previous chapters I have reviewed some key aspects of archaeology and archaeological practice and occasionally pointed to reasons for the popularity of both archaeology and its subject matter: the past and its remains. But one overriding question remains to be dealt with in more detail: what is it that makes archaeology so extraordinary and appealing in our society? In this chapter, I propose that the answer lies in the special "archaeo-appeal," doubly manifested in doing archaeology and in imagining life in the past. In other words, the popular appeal of archaeological methodology, sites, and artifacts is less due to some subtle characteristics of the source material or the subject matter and relies more on broader aesthetic experiences and metaphors.

Why Zoos Are Fun

A general trend away from valuing "pure" objects and towards broader experiences is typical of many themed environments, among them, contemporary zoos. Looking at zoos can provide a number of important insights that have relevance also to archaeology.

Besides their serious roles in preservation and education, modern zoos are very much about family entertainment, and it is this aspect especially that accounts for their enormous popularity. People visit zoos not to learn about animals, but to have a good time and talk to each other about the animals. Scott Montgomery (1995: 575) states correctly that "if the zoo were about learning, in any institutional sense, no one would go."

In recent years, many zoos have started to theme the way they exhibit animals and to display them in metaphorical rather than literal terms. Popular themes include the jungle/rainforest, the African savannah, and the zoo as conservation center. The ever-popular exotic scenarios with crumbling ruins or ancient architecture, as well as the now increasingly seen conservationists riding in jeeps on rescue missions, rely in part on imagery that is familiar to archaeologists (see figures 9.1 and 9.2; cf. Sanes 1996–2000a). Here, we encounter again the hero who braves adversity in foreign lands in his hunt for treasured objects (animals, artifacts). Disney's Animal Kingdom near Disney World in Florida provides, for instance, the Kilimanjaro Safari through a simulated Africa. The journey takes an unexpected turn when the driver asks his passengers whether he should try to catch some poachers that have just been spotted from an airplane. A chase ensues through dense vegetation with machine-gun fire in the air, until they reach the poachers' camp where guards arrest the villains

Figure 9.1   Who comes through the jungle? Indiana Jones? Lara Croft? Or an animal conservationist? Seen in the San Diego Wild Animal Park. Photograph by Cornelius Holtorf, 2000.

Figure 9.2 An Egyptian temple with hieroglyphic murals adds "archaeo-appeal" to Antwerp Zoo, Belgium. Built in 1856, it is used for the elephants. Photograph by Cornelius Holtorf, 2003.

and the riders emerge as ecoheroes (cf. Sanes 1996–2000b). There are other ways, too, in which visitors are encouraged to take part in "scientific" research. The new Erlebnis Zoo Hannover in Germany features a stranded jeep before visitors get to the empty camp of a primatologist's field site next to the gorilla enclosure. At the Boneyard in Disney's Animal Kingdom, children are invited to "dig up the bones of a woolly mammoth in the dig site." Similar dinosaur excavations are evoked at many other zoos.

As a consequence of foregrounding exciting experiences, zoos now compete successfully with popular attractions such as themed adventure parks and (natural) heritage attractions. In some cases, such as Disney's Animal Kingdom and various Sea World theme parks in the United States, Furuviksparken near Gävle in Sweden, the already-mentioned Hannover Zoo in Germany, and Chessington World of Adventures in the United Kingdom, it is in fact difficult to draw the line between these formerly distinct categories (e.g., Sanes 1996–2000b; Davis 1995; Reichenbach 2000). They all keep exotic animals, and they all provide professional family entertainment. Given such trends, which may be described as a general "Disneyization" of family attractions, Alan Beardsworth and Alan Bryman suspect that the exhibition of animals might become subordinate to the staging of elaborate quasifications of the wild: "Rather than the animals being the primary attraction, the settings themselves will become the main objects of the visitor's entranced and admiring gaze" (2001: 100).

The design of many animal cages and enclosures gives the impression that a natural habitat has been imitated for the benefit of the animals. But ever since Carl Hagenbeck's innovations in enclosure design, it is in fact the visitors who were addressed by most of the scenery in which the animals are set while they are publicly visible, whereas backstage the animals have continuously been kept in very different conditions (see Berger 1980: 21–24; Croke 1997: 76–83; Mullan and Marvin 1999: 46–53, 78–79). This public scenery can occasionally have a strong historical dimension. The Wildwood Trust in Kent, England, for example, offers "an ancient woodland that dates back to the Domesday Book" and is now the home of animal species that "feature in ancient Saxon and Viking legends" and British folklore, such as wild boars, wolves, badgers, and ravens (www .wildwoodtrust.org).

Besides contributing to conservation schemes and joining scientific expeditions, zoos are expected to display appealing animals. There are a number of distinctive animal appeals resulting from cuteness, anthropomorphism, beauty, exoticness, or potential danger (Croke 1997: 95–100). Zoo settings, which used to be created to simply house the animals, are increasingly designed to actively facilitate the visitor's sensations of such animal appeals. Touching cute animals, imitating those which remind us of humans, marveling at beautiful species, smelling exotic scents, and hearing dangerous creatures move or groan are what a successful zoo visit is all about.

The zoologist and writer Desmond Morris (1967) once investigated the various animal appeals of different species in a large survey involving eighty thousand British schoolchildren. He found that the popularity of an animal correlated directly with the number of anthropomorphic features it possessed, such as hair, rounded outlines, flat faces, facial expressions, the ability to manipulate small objects, and vertical posture (cf. Mullan and Marvin 1999: 134). It is no surprise then that over 97 percent of the children named a mammal of some kind as their favorite animal, and the six most popular animals were chimpanzees, monkeys, horses, bushbabies, pandas, and bears. Conversely, the most hated animals lacked such anthropomorphic features: snakes, spiders, and crocodiles. Relative to age groups, Morris found that, on the whole, younger children preferred the bigger animals, while older children preferred smaller ones. The explanatory interpretation he offered was that the smaller children viewed the animals as parent substitutes, and the older children looked upon them as child substitutes (Morris 1967: 226–38; see also Mullan and Marvin 1999: 24–28). The only exception to this rule was the horse, which was found to be especially popular among girls at the onset of puberty. Although some of Morris's explanations may sound simplistic and crude, it is a fact that both animal-conservation programs and zoo displays are particularly geared towards large mammals, in general, and a few especially enigmatic species, known as "charismatic megafauna," in particular (cf. Croke 1997: 181–85). This may have something to do with the reason people visit zoos: the encounter with charismatic wild animals.

The writer and critic John Berger (1980: 19) famously claims, "The zoo to which people go to meet animals, to observe them, to see them, is, in fact a monument to the impossibility of such encounters" and, thus, a necessary disappointment. But in a recent book titled *The Modern Ark*, Vicki Croke suggests that a "mysterious link between humans and animals" is made frequently in zoos (1997: 250), and that corresponds with my own experiences, too. Croke writes, "the visitor will almost always remember an intimate connection, a brief moment when the zoo animal looked up, followed or reached out. . . . That's a magic that no camcorder or satellite can compete with" (1997: 250).

Similarly, Susan Davis (1995) discusses in her work on the Sea World theme parks how the show presentations of the killer whale Shamu try to establish emotional encounters of people with the other world of nature by successfully evoking feelings of awe, wonder, and joy. As Davis notes, some animals like Shamu appear to look back at the visitor, creating "magic moments" (see also Mulland and Marvin 1999: 19–23). The same special experience of making contact with an animal can be observed in children's zoos, where the children may pet some animals. It is this thrill of experiencing charismatic wild animals close up that is the core of the zoo experience.

What Is Archaeo-appeal?

The message from zoos to archaeology is that a simulated participation in scientific practice and the magic of encountering enigmatic objects can provide visitors with very powerful experiences. They are even stronger when they are a part of themed environments that tell exciting stories, involving the visitor in metaphorical scenarios. These experiences are entertaining, but as visitors relate their impressions immediately to themselves, they can also be highly educational.

Archaeology is increasingly recognized as ideally suited for providing precisely these kinds of magical experiences through the encounter with both a fascinating scientific discipline and the remains of past human beings (see figure 9.2). A perfect example is JORVIK, the Viking age attraction in York in northern England (www.jorvik-viking-centre.co.uk, accessed October 4, 2004). Not presenting itself as a museum, but instead providing a ride into a fully reconstructed Viking town at the very site where it once stood and illuminating some of the underlying archaeological methods and techniques, JORVIK has attracted a staggering fourteen million visitors since it opened in 1984. It effectively pays now in perpetuity for the ambitious archaeological program of the York Archaeological Trust. Similarly, the Vasa Museum in Stockholm has become Scandinavia's most popular museum by displaying the huge charismatic ship together with explanations about both its historical context and the archaeological salvage and conservation process undertaken since 1961 (www.vasamuseet.se, accessed October 4, 2004). Other attractions address the public taste for archaeology in different ways, such as Disneyland, which embraced the broad appeal of Indiana Jones by theming its currently most popular ride about one of his archaeological film adventures.

> **Thesis 12:**
> Experiencing archaeological practice and imagining the past constitute the magic of archaeology.

Themed environments that draw on archaeological themes can be found in zoos, theme parks, commercial heritage attractions, restaurants, hotels, and shopping malls. They usually provide archaeological magic in much purer form than those attractions created by professional archaeolo-

155

gists and are therefore particularly interesting for understanding archaeology's significance in popular culture. For example, one of the attractions of the Chessington World of Adventures is Tomb Blaster, which is also designed around the Indiana Jones theme (but without any of the trademarks) and involves the visitor shooting with laser guns. If you follow the evolutionary path at Hannover Zoo, you pass a simulated archaeological excavation site complete with skulls on a workbench and even a cave inhabited by a family of Neanderthals, before reaching the gorillas (Reichenbach 2000). Similarly, Furuviksparken in Sweden includes an adventure and education area dedicated to the well-known, but fictitious, Stone Age family Hedenhös, and the English Wildwood Trust is now planning to erect an entire reconstructed Saxon settlement. Behind this trend lies what might be called a particular archaeo-appeal that has long been associated with the image of the archaeologist, archaeological methodology, and archaeological subject matter as a whole (see also DeBoer 1999).

Archaeo-appeal is what makes people experience the magic of archaeology. That magic is to a large extent about the hero who travels into exotic settings and makes fantastic discoveries, usually underground, of authentic ancient objects that seem to bring him or her a little closer to the ancient people who originally made them and that sometimes, it seems, look back at us like Shamu. One important reason for archaeology's general popularity and appeal is, then, that it embodies a number of very popular motifs of Western popular culture. Archaeology combines potent contemporaneous themes such as (scientific) progress, technological wizardry, and ever more "novel" discoveries, with nostalgia for ancient worlds, Utopias, and fantastic settings in exotic locations. Not coincidentally, these are precisely the themes out of which the fantasies of Hollywood, Las Vegas, and other themed environments are made (see Gottdiener 1997: 151–52). And arguably, academic archaeology succeeds as a discipline because it, too, is good in linking itself to some of the same themes, whether deliberately or accidentally.

Curiously, many archaeological exhibitions, displays, and presentations appear to rely on the archaeo-appeal they provide without actually addressing it explicitly. More often than not, they attempt to teach visitors literal facts about a specific past period or about scientific methodology and ignore the fact that many people come first of all in order to experience a range of popular metaphors. The large majority of visitors do not care much about what kinds of pots and pans people used at any point in history but are keen (for various reasons) to realize a little bit of their dream of being an archaeologist investigating ancient sites and getting closer to ancient worlds from their own position in the present. Good examples are archaeological open-air museums featuring demonstrations of various ancient skills and crafts, from building longhouses to baking bread and making pots. Many such displays are presented according to high academic standards regarding the precise period represented and the tools used, but for visitors it is often the reconstructive process itself that is significant, rather than what is actually represented.

An interesting question is whether an elementary archaeo-appeal and its associated experiences are actually similar worldwide and have existed at all times or whether they are highly context dependent and restricted to the modern Western world. This question clearly calls for further historical and empirical studies. But two things are fairly clear from the outset. First, many of the themes in which archaeology is implicated today have remained essentially the same since the beginnings of archaeology as an academic field in the eighteenth century. The process of finding treasure below the surface, the adventurous character of fieldwork, the method of inferring the past from clues, and the social construction of age and authenticity, for example, are equally applicable to Heinrich Schliemann's times as to our own (see chapters 2 and 3; cf. Zintzen 1998).

Second, it is also clear that some of the innovations and social changes of recent decades in the Western world had profound effects on the issues discussed in this book. Gerhard Schulze (1993) argues that since the early 1980s we have been living in a society in which people increasingly live their lives for the experiences they can have. This could partly account for the particular boom of archaeology in recent years. Archaeology appears to offer precisely the kind of experiences that many people long for. Moreover, the contemporary mass media, the Internet, expanding tourism, and trends towards a global economy have no doubt been instrumental not only to the spread of themed environments and "Disneyization," but also to the global popularization of archaeological themes such as those contained in the Indiana Jones–type hero and the Sherlock Holmes–type detective-scholar. These trends also contribute to the rendering of sites like Stonehenge in the United Kingdom, the Italian town of Pompeii, the Acropolis of Athens in Greece, or the Egyptian pyramids into global archaeological clichés that are equally ubiquitous in the popular culture of their home countries as they are (or might be) in commercial TV or in Las Vegas. Clichés such as these enable people to make even strange things understandable, enjoyable, and relevant to their own social context in the familiar present. Accepting that the past is of the present therefore also requires an engagement with the abstractions and schemata within which the past is actually understood in the present (cf. Schulze 1993: chapter 9).

Looking back in time, it emerges that archaeology has always been deeply immersed in the specific cultural contexts within which it has been practiced (see Schnapp 1996). This insight is neither new nor particularly surprising, but its consequences are far-reaching. If the past is essentially of each present (rather than merely in each present), historians and archaeologists cannot discover the cause-and-effect relationships that created the conditions of each present in the first place. Ancient remains, rather than places that can tell us something about the actual past, become sites at which certain themes and stories of the present manifest themselves. Their pastness is no longer borne out in any actual processes and events that took place a long time ago but in how they are perceived and experienced today.

Some might consider this view of the role of the past in the present and the implied altered status of archaeology as diametrically opposed to their own opinions on what archaeologists and historians should base their work on (e.g., Maier 1981). They may even consider it politically dangerous to hold views like these because of the implied denial of our present's being part of a historical process and the resulting impossibility of explaining the present as a result of that process (e.g., Fowler 1994: 12–13). But for others, the possibility and necessity of historical change will derive much more naturally from analyzing current affairs, while explanations that rely predominantly on the present rather than the past avoid the danger of letting age and tradition stand in for rational justification.

Claiming that the past is of the present makes the past no less significant today. It paves the way for the assertion that the significance of the past is defined by all of us, rather than by the few who assume a position of intellectual authority from which they state how archaeological sites and artifacts are properly appreciated and ultimately what they really

A Very Brief Summary of the Argument

From Stonehenge to Las Vegas ranges a continuum of appealing archaeological themes. They are what this book has been about. I began with a theoretical argument that archaeology is mainly about our own culture in the present, rather than about past cultures, since what matters most about recalling the past is not whether people remember it accurately but who remembers what and how at any given point in time and space. Collective memories often imply a particular image of archaeology, and this is what I turned to next.

In popular culture, archaeology is about searching and finding treasure below the surface. The necessary fieldwork involves making discoveries under tough conditions and in exotic locations. As a detective of the past, the archaeologist tries to piece together what happened in the past. For many this process of doing archaeology is more exciting and important than its actual results. The three themes of searching for underground treasures, conducting adventurous fieldwork, and employing criminological procedures are culturally meaningful in a wide range of fields. They also come together in the aims, actions, and skills of the archaeologist and give him or her a special appeal.

Yet, as popular as archaeological practice may be, there are alternatives to it. A look at archaeological sites and artifacts in past and present shows that their meanings have varied enormously. Even today they mean very different things to different people. Often their significance is to a large extent metaphorical; that is, it does not reside in what they are but in what they are taken to be. All these meanings are equally important. Considering also that they are constantly changing, depending on who is looking at an archaeological site or artifact in what specific context, even the presumed authenticity of any such object comes to depend on the context of the observer. Perceived pastness thus becomes more important than actual age. The past is effectively remade in every present culture, and in this sense, it is a renewable resource. Archaeologists' widespread preoccupation with preservation is arguably misplaced. There are indeed cases where much can be gained from effectively destroying an ancient site.

What matters most regarding archaeology's social significance is the magic it conveys. Archaeology's very special popular appeal is based on the experiences of doing archaeology and imagining the past, both often in metaphorical terms. Such archaeo-appeal is at the heart of archaeology and its ultimate reason and justification.

This does not mean that archaeology is necessarily uncritical and without a political edge. But archaeologists should not prescribe to other people how or what to think about the past. Instead, archaeology's critical potential lies in the capacity to open people's eyes, both in amazement at the magic provided by archaeology and through insights into the characteristics and significant implications of that magic, such as those explored in this book.

mean for us. At the end of the day, professional archaeologists must provide a service for society. They are therefore well advised to consider carefully how people actually (prefer to) experience archaeology, the past, and its remains and what particular archaeo-appeal different sites and objects may offer to their audiences (see also Merriman 2002).

If archaeology is popular culture, then we are all archaeologists. That does not allow us to claim extra wages, but it does allow us to celebrate jointly the diverse meanings of archaeological sites and artifacts, from Stonehenge to Las Vegas, and to enjoy together the visions, thrills, and desires of doing archaeology. As I hope to have shown throughout this book, archaeology can create exciting and insightful moments in our lives. At its best it lets us sense the magic that can be derived from the experiences of both archaeological research and the past.

BIBLIOGRAPHY

Arnesen, Britt. 2001. Blood, sweat, and DEET: field archaeology in the Alaskan interior, available at netproz.com/britt/arnesen.txt (accessed November 16, 2001).

Ascher, Robert. 1960. Archaeology and the public image. *American Antiquity* 25:402–403.

Bagnall, Gaynor. 1996. Consuming the past. In *Consumption Matters: The Production and Experience of Consumption*, ed. S. Edgell, K. Hetherington, and A. Wade, 227–47. Oxford: Blackwell.

Barner, W. 1957. Von Kultäxten, Beilzauber und rituellem Bohren. *Die Kunde* N. F. 8:175–86.

Barrett, John. 1994. *Fragments from Antiquity: An Archaeology of Social Life in Britain, 2900–1200* BC. Oxford: Blackwell.

Bausinger, Hermann, Utz Jeggle, Gottfried Korff, and Martin Scharfe, 1978. *Grundzüge der Volkskunde*. Darmstadt: Wissenschaftliche Buchgesellschaft.

Beardsworth, Alan, and Alan Bryman. 1999. Late modernity and the dynamics of quasification: the case of the themed restaurant. *The Sociological Review* 47:228–57.

———. 2001. The wild animal in late modernity: the case of the Disneyization of zoos. *Tourist Studies* 1:83–104.

Beavan, Colin. 2002. *Fingerprints: Murder and the Race to Uncover the Science of Identity*. London: Fourth Estate.

Bender, Barbara. 1998. *Stonehenge: Making Space*. Oxford: Berg.

Benjamin, Walter. 1992. The work of art in the age of mechanical reproduction [1936]. In *Illuminations*, 211–44. London: Fontana. Also available at www.marxists.org/reference/subject/philosophy/works/ge/benjamin.htm (accessed September 24, 2004).

Berger, John. 1980. Why look at animals? In *About Looking*, 1–26. London: Writers and Readers.

Bergman, Charles. 2002. Inventing a beast with no body: radiotelemetry, wildlife biology, and the simulation of ecology. Paper presented at the annual conference of the International Society for Anthrozoology, London, August 19–21, 2002. Publication forthcoming in the journal *Worldviews*.

Bernfeld, Suzanne Cassirer. 1951. Freud and archaeology. *American Imago* 5: 107–28.

Bibby, Geoffrey. 1957. *The Testimony of the Spade*. London: Collins.

Blinkenberg, Christian. 1911. *The Thunderweapon in Religion and Folklore: A Study in Comparative Archaeology*. Cambridge: Cambridge University Press.

Borbein, Adolf. 1981. Archäologie und historisches Bewußtsein. In *Archäologie und Gesellschaft: Forschung und öffentliches Interesse*, ed. B. Andreae, 45–76. Stuttgart: Wissenschaftliche Verlagsgesellschaft.

Bradley, Richard. 1993. *Altering the Earth: The Origins of Monuments in Britain and Continental Europe*. Edinburgh: Society of Antiquaries of Scotland.

Bruner, Edward. 1994. Abraham Lincoln as authentic reproduction: a critique of postmodernism. *American Anthropologist* 96:397–415.

Bryman, Alan. 1999. The Disneyization of society. *The Sociological Review* 47:25–47.

Burroughs, Edgar Rice. 2000. *At the Earth's Core* [1914]. Afterword by Phillip Burger. Lincoln and London: University of Nebraska Press.

Butler, Samuel. 2002. *Hudibras* [1663]. Project Gutenberg online edition, available at www.gutenberg.net/browse/BIBREC/BR4937.HTM (accessed September 24, 2004).

Byrne, Denis. 1991. Western hegemony in archaeological heritage management. *History and Anthropology* 5:269–76.

———. 1995. Buddhist *stupa* and Thai social practice. *World Archaeology* 27:266–88.

Cahill, Tim. 1981. The fighting archaeologist: tearing up the American West and putting it back together again with Dr. Larry Lahren. *Outside* (November):36–39, 73–76.

Carelli, Peter. 1997. Thunder and lightning, magical miracles: on the popular myth of thunderbolts and the presence of Stone Age artefacts in medieval deposits. In *Visions of the Past: Trends and Traditions in Swedish Medieval Archaeology*, eds. H. Andersson, P. Carelli, and L. Ersgård, 393–417. Stockholm: Almqvist and Wiksell.

Carman, John. 1996. *Valuing Ancient Things: Archaeology and Law*. London: Leicester University Press.

Ceram, C. W. 1980. *Gods, Graves and Scholars: The Story of Archaeology* [first published in German in 1949]. Harmondsworth: Penguin.

Chippindale, Christopher. 1994. *Stonehenge Complete*. Revised edition. London: Thames and Hudson.

Chippindale, Christopher, Paul Devereux, Peter Fowler, Rhys Jones, and Tim Sebastian. 1990. *Who Owns Stonehenge?* London: Batsford.

Christie, Agatha. 1960. *Death on the Nile* [1937]. London: Fontana/Collins.

———. 1977. *An Autobiography*. London: Collins.

———. 1994. *Murder in Mesopotamia* [1936]. London: HarperCollins.

Cleal, Rosamund, K. Walker, and R. Montague. 1995. *Stonehenge in its Landscape: Twentieth Century Excavations*. London: English Heritage.

Cohen, Eric. 1988. Authenticity and commoditization in tourism. *Annals of Tourism Research* 15:371–86.

Cohodas, Marvin. 2003. A new heroics of archaeology. Paper presented at the Fifth World Archaeological Congress, Washington, D.C., June 2003, available at godot.unisa.edu.au/wac/pdfs/213.pdf (accessed September 24, 2004).

Cole, John. 1980. Cult archaeology and unscientific method and theory. *Advances in Archaeological Method and Theory* 3:1–33.

Coles, Alex, and Mark Dion Hrsg. 1999. *Mark Dion: Archaeology*. Black Dog Publishing.

Cooney, Gabriel. 2000. *Landscapes of Neolithic Ireland*. London: Routledge.

Cooper, Malcolm, Antony Firth, John Carman, and David Wheatley, eds. 1995. *Managing Archaeology*. London: Routledge.

Corrin, Lisa, Miwon Kwon, and Norman Bryson. 1997. *Mark Dion*. London: Phaidon.

Cox, Margaret. 2001. Forensic archaeology in the UK: Questions of socio-intellectual context and socio-political responsibility. In *Archaeologies of the Contemporary Past*, eds. V. Buchli and G. Lucas, 145–57. London: Routledge.

Cresswell, Tim. 1996. *In Place/Out of Place: Geography, Ideology, and Transgression*. Minneapolis and London: University of Minnesota Press.

Croke, Vicki. 1997. *The Modern Ark: The Story of Zoos: Past, Present and Future*. New York: Avon.

Daniel, Glyn. 1972. *Megaliths in History*. London: Thames and Hudson.

Darvill, Timothy. 1993. "Can nothing compare 2 U?" Resources and philosophies in archaeological resource management and beyond. In *Rescuing the Historic Environment: Archaeology, the Green Movement and Conservation Strategies for the British Landscape*, ed. H. Swain, 5–8. Hertford: RESCUE, The British Archaeological Trust.

Darvill, Timothy, and Andrew K. Fulton. 1998. *The Monuments at Risk Survey of England 1995: Summary Report*. London: English Heritage.

Darvill, Timothy, Katherine Barker, Barbara Bender, and Ronald Hutton. 1999. *The Cerne Giant: An Antiquity on Trial*. Oxford: Oxbow.

Davis, Susan G. 1995. Touch the magic. In *Uncommon Ground: Toward Reinventing Nature*, ed. W. Cronon, 204–17. New York: Norton & Co.

Day, David. 1997. *A Treasure Hard to Attain: Images of Archaeology in Popular Film, with a Filmography.* Lanham, MD: Scarecrow Press.

DeBoer, Warren. 1999. Metaphors we dig by. *Anthropology News* (October):7–8.

Dickson, Jane. 1993. Who's afraid of the big bad mouse? *The Sunday Times Magazine,* March 28, 30–34.

Dion, Mark. 1997. *Natural History and Other Fictions.* Exhibition catalogue: Ikon Gallery Birmingham, Kunstverein Hamburg, De Appel Amsterdam.

Dyson, Stephen L. 2001. Rome in America. In *Images of Rome: Perceptions of Ancient Rome in Europe and the Unites States in the Modern Age,* ed. R. Hingley, 57–69. *Journal of Roman Archaeology,* supplementary series 44.

Ebeling, Knut. 2004. Die Mumie kehrt zurück II. Zur Aktualität des Archäologischen in Wissenschaft, Kunst und Medien. In *Die Aktualität des Archäologischen,* eds. K. Ebeling and S. Altekamp, pp. 9–30. Frankfurt: Fischer.

Eco, Umberto. 1986. *Travels in Hyperreality.* San Diego: Harcourt Brace Jovanovich.

———. 1990. Fakes and forgeries [1986]. In U. Eco, *The Limits of Interpretation,* 174–202. Bloomington: Indiana University Press.

Edgeworth, Matthew. 1990. Analogy as practical reason: the perception of objects in excavation practice. *Archaeological Review from Cambridge* 9:243–51.

———. 2003. *Acts of Discovery: An Ethnography of Archaeological Practice.* BAR Int. Ser. 1131. Oxford: Archaeopress.

Edwards, Brian. 2000. Avebury and other not-so-ancient places: the making of the English heritage landscape. In *Seeing History: Public History in Britain Now,* eds. H. Kean, P. Martin, and S. Morgan, 65–79. London: Francis Boutle.

Eliade, Mircea. 1962. *The Forge and the Crucible.* London: Rider & Co.

Evans-Pritchard, Deirdre. 1993. Ancient art in modern context. *Annals of Tourism Research* 20:9–31.

Feder, Kenneth. 1999. *Frauds, Myths and Mysteries: Science and Pseudoscience in Archaeology.* 3rd ed. Mountain View: Mayfield.

Fehr, Burkhart. 1992. Nicht Museum, nicht Disneyland. Zur Problematik archäologischer Parks in Mitteleuropa. In *Antike heute,* eds. R. Faber and B. Kytzler, 54–67. Würzburg: Königshausen & Neumann.

Fentress, James, and Chris Wickham. 1992. *Social Memory.* Oxford: Blackwell.

Fiske, John. 1989. *Reading the Popular.* London: Routledge.

Fjellman, Stephen. 1992. *Vinyl Leaves: Walt Disney World and America.* Boulder, CO: Westview.

Flaig, Egon. 1999. Spuren des Ungeschehenen. Warum die bildende Kunst der

Geschichtswissenschaft nicht helfen kann. In *Archäologie zwischen Imagination und Wissenschaft: Anne und Patrick Poirier*, ed. B. Jussen, 16–50. Göttingen: Wallstein.

Fletcher, Edward. 1973. *Treasure Hunting for All: A Popular Guide to a Profitable Hobby*. London: Blandford.

Fluck, Winfried. 1987. Popular culture as a mode of socialization: a theory about the social functions of popular cultural forms. *Journal of Popular Culture* 21:31–46.

Foucault, Michel. 1970. *The Order of Things* [1966]. London: Routledge.

———. 1992. *The Archaeology of Knowledge* [1969]. London: Routledge.

Fowler, Peter. 1994. The nature of the times deceas'd. *International Journal of Heritage Studies* 1:6–17.

Franz, Leonhard. 1931. "Selbstgewachsene" Altertümer. *Wiener prähistorische Zeitschrift* 18:10–21.

Frayling, Christopher. 1992. *The Face of Tutankhamun*. London and Boston: Faber and Faber.

Freud, Sigmund. 1961. Lecture II: parapraxes [1915]. In *The Standard Edition of the Complete Psychological Works of Sigmund Freud*, Vol. 15, ed. J. Strachey, 25–39. London: Hogarth.

———. 1964. Constructions in analysis [1937]. In *The Standard Edition of the Complete Psychological Works of Sigmund Freud*, Vol. 23, ed. J. Strachey, 255–69. London: Hogarth.

Fritz, J. M. 1973. Relevance, archaeology and subsistence theory. In *Research and Theory in Current Archaeology*, ed. C. Redman, 59–82. New York: Wiley & Sons.

Gazin-Schwartz, Amy, and Cornelius Holtorf, eds. 1999. *Archaeology and Folklore*. London: Routledge.

Gere, Cathy. 2002. Inscribing nature: archaeological metaphors and the formation of new sciences. *Public Archaeology* 2:195–208.

Gero, Joan. 1996. Archaeological practice and gendered encounters with field data. In *Gender and Archaeology*, ed. R. Wright, 251–80. Philadelphia: University of Pennsylvania Press.

Gero, Joan, and Dolores Root. 1990. Public presentations and private concerns: archeology in the pages of the National Geographic. In *The Politics of the Past*, eds. P. Gathercole and D. Lowenthal, 19–37. London: Unwin Hyman.

Ginzburg, Carlo. 1983. Morelli, Freud and Sherlock Holmes: clues and scientific method [1979]. In *The Sign of Three: Dupin, Holmes, Peirce*, eds. U. Eco and T. A. Sebeok, 81–118. Bloomington: Indiana University Press.

Gottdiener, Mark. 1997. *The Theming of America: Dreams, Visions and Commercial Spaces*. Boulder, CO: Westview Press.

BIBLIOGRAPHY

Gould, Stephen Jay. 1987. *Time's Arrow, Time's Cycle: Myth and Metaphor in the Discovery of Geological Time*. Harmondsworth: Penguin.

Grinsell, Leslie. 1967. Barrow treasure, in fact, tradition and legislation. *Folklore* 78:1–38.

———. 1976. *Folklore of Prehistoric Sites in Britain*. London: David & Charles Gustafsson, Lotten. 2002. *Den förtrollande zonen: Lekar med tid, rum och identitet under Medeltidsveckan på Gotland*. Nora: Nya Doxa.

Hall, Martin. 2001. Cape Town's District Six and the archaeology of memory. In *Destruction and Conservation of Cultural Property*, eds. R. Layton, P. Stone, and J. Thomas, 298–311. London: Routledge.

Hawkes, Jacquetta. 1967. God in the machine. *Antiquity* 41:174–80.

Heid, Klaus. 1995–2000. *Khuza. Ein Mythos aus Sibirien*. Online catalogue and documentation, archived at web.archive.org/web/20040205115152/www.tuareg.de/khuza.

Hennig, Christoph. 1999. *Reiselust. Touristen, Tourismus und Urlaubskultur*. Frankfurt: Suhrkamp.

Hill, Tobias. 1999. *Underground*. London: Faber and Faber.

Himmelmann, Nikolaus. 1976. *Utopische Vergangenheit: Archäologie und moderne Kultur*. Berlin: Gebr. Mann.

Hingley, Richard. 1996. Ancestors and identity in the later prehistory of Atlantic Scotland: the reuse and reinvention of Neolithic monuments and material culture. *World Archaeology* 28:231–43.

Hirst, Kris. 1998. A lesson in applied archaeology: an interview with Clark Erickson, available at archaeology.about.com/cs/agriculture/a/erickson1.htm (accessed September 24, 2004).

Hjemdahl, Kirsti Mathiesen. 2002. History as a cultural playground. *Ethnologia Europaea* 32:105–24.

Holtorf, Christian. 2001. Der erste Draht zur neuen Welt. Eine Archäologie der Zukunft. In *Mythos Neanderthal: Ursprung und Zeitenwende*, eds. D. Matejovski, D. Kamper and G. Weniger, 86–97. Frankfurt: Campus.

Holtorf, Cornelius. 2000–2004. *Monumental Past: The Life-histories of Megalithic Monuments in Mecklenburg-Vorpommern (Germany)*. Electronic monograph. University of Toronto: Centre for Instructional Technology Development, available at http://hdl.handle.net/1807/245 (accessed September 24, 2004).

———. 2002. Notes on the life history of a pot sherd. *Journal of Material Culture* 7:49–71.

———. Forthcoming. Studying archaeological fieldwork in the field: views from Monte Polizzo. In *Ethnographies of Archaeology*, ed. M. Edgeworth. Walnut Creek, CA: AltaMira.

Hopkins, Jeffrey. 1990. West Edmonton Mall: landscape of myths and else-whereness. *The Canadian Geographer* 34:2–17.

Hunter, John, Charlotte Roberts, and Anthony Martin. 1996. *Studies in Crime: An Introduction to Forensic Archaeology.* London: Batsford.

Huxley, Thomas. 1880. On the method of Zadig: retrospective prophecy as a function of science. In *Science and Hebrew Tradition*, Vol. 4 of *Collected Essays*, 1–23, London: Macmillan. Also available at aleph0.clarku.edu/huxley/CE4/Zadig.html (accessed September 24, 2004).

James, Simon. 2001. The Roman galley slave. Ben-Hur and the birth of a factoid. *Public Archaeology* 2:35–49.

Jensen, Ola. 1999. From divine missiles to human implements: the shift in the perception of antiquities during the second half of the 17th century. In *Glyfer och arkeologiska rum—en vänbok till Jarl Nordbladh*, eds. A. Gustafsson and H. Karlsson, 553–67. University of Göteborg, Institute of Archaeology.

Jensen, Inken, and Alfried Wieczorek, eds. 2002. *Dino, Zeus und Asterix: Zeitzeuge Archäologie in Werbung, Kunst und Alltag heute.* Mannheim: Reiss-Engelhorn-Museen and Langenweißbach: Beier & Beran.

Johnson, Mark. 2001. Renovating Hue (Vietnam): authenticating destruction, reconstructing authenticity. In *Destruction and Conservation of Cultural Property*, eds. R. Layton, P. Stone, J. Thomas, 75–92. London: Routledge.

Jokilehto, Jukka. 1995. Authenticity: a general framework for the concept. In *Nara Conference on Authenticity*, ed. K. E. Larsen, 17–34. Trondheim: Tapir.

Jones, Andrew. 2002. *Archaeological Theory and Scientific Practice.* Cambridge: Cambridge University Press.

Jungk, Robert. 2000. The ruins complex [1981]. In M. Hamm and R. Steinberg, *Dead Tech: A Guide to the Archaeology of Tomorrow*, 7–10. Santa Monica, CA: Hennessey & Ingalls.

Jussen, Bernhard, ed. 1999. *Archäologie zwischen Imagination und Wissenschaft: Anne und Patrick Poirier.* Göttingen: Wallstein.

Kaiser, David. 1998. Stonehenge: American style. *3rd Stone* 32:31–32.

Kalinowski, Konstanty. 1993. Der Wiederaufbau der historischen Stadtzentren in Polen—Theoretische Voraussetzungen und Realisation am Beispiel Danzigs. In *Denkmal—Werte—Gesellschaft: zur Pluralität des Denkmalbegriffs*, ed. W. Lipp, 322–46. Frankfurt: Campus.

Kemper, Steven. 1991. *The Presence of the Past. Chronicles, Politics, and Culture in Sinhala Life.* Ithaca, NY: Cornell University Press.

Kidder, A. 1949. Introduction. In C. Amsden, *Prehistoric Southwesterners from Basketmaker to Pueblo*, xi–xiv. Los Angeles: Southwest Museum.

King, Thomas, Randall Jacobson, Karen Burns, and Kenton Spading. 2001.

Amelia Earhart's Shoes: Is the Mystery Solved? Walnut Creek: AltaMira Press. See also www.tighar.org/Projects/Earhart/AEoverview.html (accessed September 24, 2004).

Knight, Anna. 1999. *The Lost Temple: An Interactice Puzzle Storybook.* London: Dorling Kindersley.

Köck, Christoph. 1990. *Sehnsucht Abenteuer: Auf den Spuren der Erlebnisgesellschaft.* Berlin: Transit.

Kopytoff, Igor. 1986. The cultural biography of things: commoditization as process. In *The Social Life of Things: Commodities in Cultural Perspective,* ed. A. Appadurai, 64–91. Cambridge: Cambridge University Press.

Korte, Barbara. 2000. 'The Reassuring Science'? Archäologie als Sujet und Metapher in der Literatur Britanniens. *Poetica* 32:125–50.

Krämer, Anja. 1999. Die unfreiwillige Serie—wiederholte Wiederaufbauten im Umfeld der Denkmalpflege. Lecture given as part of the Thealit-Laboratorium "Serialität: Reihen und Netze," available at www.thealit.dsn.de/lab/serialitaet/teil/kraemer/kraemer1.html (accessed September 24, 2004).

Krieger, Martin. 1973. What's wrong with plastic trees? *Science* 179 (February 2):446–55.

Kristiansen, Kristian. 1993. "The past and its great might": an essay on the use of the past. *Journal of European Archaeology* 1:3–32.

Kuspit, Donald. 1989. A mighty metaphor: the analogy of archaeology and psychoanalysis. In *Sigmund Freud and Art: His Personal Collection of Antiquities,* ed. P. Gay, 132–51. London: Thames and Hudson.

Lakoff, George, and Mark Johnson. 1980. *Metaphors We Live By.* Chicago and London: University of Chicago Press.

Larsen, Knut, ed. 1995. *Nara Conference on Authenticity.* Trondheim: Tapir.

Latour, Bruno. 1983. Give me a laboratory and I will raise the world. In *Science Observed,* eds. Karin Knorr-Cetina and Michael Mulkay, 141–70. London: Sage.

Layton, Robert, ed. 1994. *Who Needs the Past? Indigenous Values and Archaeology.* London: Routledge.

Layton, Robert, Peter Stone, and Julian Thomas, eds. 2001. *Destruction and Conservation of Cultural Property.* London: Routledge.

Leone, Mark, and Parker Potter Jr. 1992. Legitimation and the classification of archaeological sites. *American Antiquity* 57:137–45.

Leppmann, Wolfgang. 1966. *Pompeii in Fact and Fiction.* London: Elek.

Lesser, Wendy. 1987. *The Life below the Ground: A Study of the Subterranean in Literature and History.* Boston: Faber and Faber.

Liebers, Claudia. 1986. *Neolithische Megalithgräber in Volksglauben und Volksleben:*

Untersuchung historischer Quellen zur Volksüberlieferung, zum Denkmalschutz und zur Fremdenverkehrswerbung. Frankfurt: Lang.

Lindqvist, Sven. 1978. *Gräv där du står: hur man utforskar ett jobb.* Stockholm: Bonnier.

Löhlein, Wolfgang. 2003. Majestät brauchen Scherben. *Antike Welt* 34:659–64.

Lomborg, Bjørn. 2001. *The Skeptical Environmentalist: Measuring the Real State of the World.* Cambridge: Cambridge University Press.

Loukatos, Demetrios. 1978. Tourist archaeofolklore in Greece. In *Folklore in the Modern World*, ed. R. Dorson, 175–82. The Hague: Mouton.

Lowenthal, David. 1985. *The Past Is a Foreign Country.* Cambridge: Cambridge University Press.

———. 1992. Authenticity? the dogma of self-delusion. In *Why Fakes Matter: Essays on Problems of Authenticity*, ed. M. Jones, 184–92. London: British Museum Press.

———. 1994. Criteria of authenticity. In *Conference on Authenticity in Relation to the World Heritage Convention: Proceedings of the Preparatory Workshop in Bergen, Norway, 31 January–2 February 1994*, eds. K. E. Larsen and N. Marstein, 35–64. Oslo: Riksantikvaren.

———. 1998. Fabricating heritage. *History and Memory* 10:5–24.

Lucas, Gavin. 1997. Forgetting the past. *Anthropology Today* 13, no. 1 (February):8–14.

———. 2001a. *Critical Approaches to Fieldwork. Contemporary and Historical Archaeological Practice.* London: Routledge.

———. 2001b. Destruction and the rhetoric of excavation. *Norwegian Archaeological Review* 34:35–46.

Maase, Kaspar, and Bernd J. Warneken, eds. 2003. *Unterwelten der Kultur: Themen und Theorien der volkskundlichen Kulturwissenschaft.* Köln: Böhlau.

Macaulay, David. 1976. *Underground.* Boston: Houghton Mifflin.

MacCannell, Dean. 1973. Staged authenticity: arrangements of social space in tourist settings. *American Journal of Sociology* 79, no. 3:589–603.

Maier, Franz G. 1981. Archäologie und moderne Welt. In *Archäologie und Gesellschaft: Forschung und öffentliches Interesse*, ed. B. Andreae, 31–44. Stuttgart: Wissenschaftliche Verlagsgesellschaft.

Malamud, Margaret. 1998. As the Romans did? Theming ancient Rome in contemporary Las Vegas. *Arion*, 3rd series, 6, no. 2:11–39.

———. 2001. Pyramids in Las Vegas and in outer space: ancient Egypt in twentieth-century American architecture and film. *Journal of Popular Culture* 34:31–47.

Maltby, Richard. 1989. Introduction. In *Dreams for Sale: Popular Culture in the 20th Century*, ed. R. Maltby, 8–19. London: Harrap.

BIBLIOGRAPHY

Martinón-Torres, Marcos. 2002. Defying God and the king. A 17th-century gold rush for "megalithic treasure." *Public Archaeology* 2:219–35.

McCombie, Mel. 2001. Art appreciation at Caesar's Palace. In *Popular Culture: Production and Consumption*, eds. C. Harrington and D. Bielby, 53–63. Oxford: Blackwell.

Mead, George H. 1929. The nature of the past. In *Essays in Honor of John Dewey*, ed. J. Coss, 235–42. New York: Henry Holt.

Membury, Steven. 2002. The celluloid archaeologist—an x-rated exposé. In *Digging Holes in Popular Culture. Archaeology and Science Fiction*, ed. M. Russell, 8–18. Oxford: Oxbow/The David Brown Book Company.

Merchant, Carolyn. 1980. *The Death of Nature: Women, Ecology and the Scientific Revolution*. San Francisco: Harper & Row.

Merriman, Nick. 2002. Archaeology, heritage and interpretation. In *Archaeology. The Widening Debate*, eds. B. Cunliffe, W. Davies, and C. Renfrew, 541–66. Oxford: Oxford University Press.

Mertens, Wolfgang, and Rolf Haubl. 1996. *Der Psychoanalytiker als Archäologe*. Stuttgart: Kohlhammer.

Metken, Günter. 1977. *Spurensicherung. Kunst als Anthropologie und Selbsterforschung. Fiktive Wissenschaft in der heutigen Kunst*. Köln: DuMont.

———. 1996. *Spurensicherung—Eine Revision. Texte 1977–1995*. Amsterdam: Verlag der Kunst.

Michlovic, Michael. 1990. Folk archaeology in anthropological perspective. *Current Anthropology* 31:103–7.

Middleton, David, and Derek Edwards, eds. 1990. *Collective Remembering*. London: Sage.

Mitchell, W. J. Thomas. 1998. *The Last Dinosaur Book: The Life and Times of a Cultural Icon*. London and Chicago: University of Chicago Press.

Montgomery, Scott. 1995. The zoo: theatre of the animals. *Science as Culture* 4, no. 21:565–600.

Moore, Kevin. 1997. *Museums and Popular Culture*. London: Cassel.

Moreland, John. 1999. The world(s) of the cross. *World Archaeology* 31:194–213.

Morris, Desmond. 1967. *The Naked Ape: A Zoologist's Study of the Human Animal*. London: Cape.

Moser, Stephanie. 1995. Archaeology and its disciplinary culture: the professionalisation of Australian prehistoric archaeology. Unpublished doctoral dissertation. University of Sydney.

———. 1998. *Ancestral Images: The Iconography of Human Origins*. Thrupp: Sutton.

———. Forthcoming. Gendered dimensions of archaeological practice: the stereotyping of archaeology as fieldwork. In *Practicing Archaeology as a Feminist*, eds. A. Wylie and M. Conkey. Santa Fe, NM: School of American Research.

Mullan, Bob, and Garry Marvin. 1999. *Zoo Culture: The Book about Watching People Watch Animals.* 2nd ed. Urbana: University of Illinois Press.

Myrberg, Nanouschka. 2004. False monuments? On antiquity and authenticity. *Public Archaeology* 3:151–61.

Neuhaus, Volker. 2001. The Archaeology of murder. In *Agatha Christie and Archaeology*, ed. C. Trümpler, 425–35. London: British Museum Press.

Nora, Pierre. 1989. Between memory and history: les lieux de mémoire [1984]. *Representations* 26 (Spring):7–25 (also in Nora and Kritzman 1996: 1–20).

———. 1996. From lieux de mémoire to realms of memory. In *Conflicts and Divisions*, Vol. 1 of *Realms of Memory: Rethinking the French Past*, eds. Nora and Kritzman, xv–xxiv. New York: Columbia University Press.

Nora, Pierre, ed. 1984–1992. *Les lieux de mémoire.* 7 vols. Paris: Edition Gallimard. English Edition: Nora and Kritzman eds. 1996–1998.

Nora, Pierre, and Lawrence Kritzman, eds. 1996–1998. *Realms of Memory: Rethinking the French Past.* 3 vols. New York: Columbia University Press.

Norman, Bruce. 1983. Archaeology and television. *Archaeological Review from Cambridge* 2:1, 27–32.

Oels, David. 2002. Mit hundert Sachen erzählt. Sachbuch, Literatur und die Wiederkehr des Erzählens. In *literatur.com: Tendenzen im Literaturmarketing*, ed. E. Schütz and T. Wegmann, 81–106. Berlin: Weidler.

Ouzman, Sven. 2001. Seeing is deceiving: rock art and the non-visual. *World Archaeology* 33:237–56

Pallottino, Massimo. 1968. *The Meaning of Archaeology.* London: Thames and Hudson.

Patrik, Linda. 1985. Is there an archaeological record? *Advances in Archaeological Method and Theory* 8:27–62.

Peacock, Alan. 1978. Preserving the past: an international economic dilemma. *Journal of Cultural Economics* 2, no. 2:1–11.

Pearson, Mike, and Michael Shanks. 2001. *Theatre/Archaeology.* London: Routledge.

Petersson, Bodil. 2003. *Föreställningar om det förflutna: Arkeologi och rekonstruktion.* Lund: Nordic Academic Press.

Petzet, Michael. 1995. "In the full richness of their authenticity": the test of authenticity and the new cult of monuments. In *Nara Conference on Authenticity*, ed. K. E. Larsen, 85–99. Trondheim: Tapir.

Poirier, Anne, and Patrick Poirier. 1994. *Anne et Patrick Poirier.* Exhibition catalogue: Museum Moderner Kunst Stiftung Ludwig, Wien and Le Capitou, Centre d'Art Contemporain Fréjus. Milano: Electa.

Pollock, Susan, and Catherine Lutz. 1994. Archaeology deployed for the Gulf War. *Critique of Anthropology* 14:263–84.

Pomian, Krysztof. 1996. Franks and Gauls [1992]. In *Conflicts and Divisions*, Vol. 1 of *Realms of Memory: Rethinking the French Past*, eds. L. D. Kritzman and P. Nora, 29–76. New York: Columbia University Press.

Pörtner, Rudolf. 1959. *Mit dem Fahrstuhl in die Römerzeit: Städte und Stätten deutscher Frühgeschichte.* Düsseldorf: Econ.

Predator. 1999. Approach: a sprawling manifesto on the art of drain exploring, available at www.infiltration.org/approach.htm (accessed September 24, 2004).

Pryor, Francis. 2001. *Seahenge. New Discoveries in Prehistoric Britain.* London: HarperCollins.

Putnam, James. 2001. *Art and Artifact. The Museum as Medium.* London: Thames and Hudson.

Rehork, Joachim. 1987. *Sie fanden, was sie kannten. Archäologie als Spiegel der Neuzeit.* München: Hueber.

Reichenbach, Herman. 2000. The new Hannover Zoo. *International Zoo News* 47, no. 3 (April/May): available at www.zoonews.ws/IZN/300/IZN-300 .html (accessed September 24, 2004).

Reitinger, Josef. 1976. "Donnerkeile" aus Oberösterreich und Salzburg. In *Festschrift für Richard Pittioni zum siebzigsten Geburtstag,* Vol. 2, eds. H. Mitscha-Märheim et al., 511–46. Wien: Deuticke and Horn: Berger und Söhne.

Renfrew, Colin. 2003. *Figuring It Out: The Parallel Visions of Artists and Archaeologists.* London: Thames and Hudson.

Riegl, Alois. 1982. The Modern cult of monuments: its character and its origin [1903]. *Oppositions* 25 (Fall):21–51.

Robbins, Catherine. 2001. No room for riches of the Indian past. *The New York Times,* November 24.

Robinson, Tony, and Mick Aston. 2002. *Archaeology Is Rubbish: A Beginner's Guide.* London: Channel 4 Books.

Rollins, James. 2000. *Excavation.* New York: Harpertorch.

Ross, Werner. 1980. *Die Schatzgräberwissenschaft: Faszination und Grenzen der Archäologie.* Public lecture. Main: Philipp von Zabern.

Rüsen, Jörn. 1994a. Was ist Geschichtsbewußtsein? Theoretische Überlegungen und heuristische Hinweise [1991]. In *Historische Orientierung*, 3–24. Köln: Böhlau.

———. 1994b. Geschichtskultur als Forschungsproblem [1992]. In *Historische Orientierung*, 235–45. Köln: Böhlau.

———. 1994c. Was ist Geschichtskultur? Überlegungen zu einer neuen Art, über Geschichte nachzudenken. In *Historische Faszination: Geschichtskultur heute*, eds. K. Füßmann, H. T. Grütter and J. Rüsen, 3–26. Köln: Böhlau.

Russell, Lynette. 2002. Archaeology and Star Trek: exploring the past in the future. In *Digging Holes in Popular Culture: Archaeology and Science Fiction*, ed. M. Russell, 19–29. Oxford: Oxbow/The David Brown Book Company.

Russell, Miles. 2002. "No more heroes any more": the dangerous world of the pop culture archaeologist. In *Digging Holes in Popular Culture: Archaeology and Science Fiction*, ed. M. Russell, 38–54. Oxford: Oxbow/The David Brown Book Company.

Samuel, Raphael. 1994. *Theatres of Memory: Past and Present in Contemporary Culture*. London: Verso.

Sanes, Ken. 1996–2000a. Zoos, rain forest exhibits and simulation: worlds in a bottle, available at www.transparencynow.com/rainforest.htm (accessed September 4, 2004).

———. 1996–2000b. Disney's distorted mirror, available at www.transparencynow.com/Disney/distable1.htm (accessed September 24, 2004).

Schiffer, Michael, with Andrea Miller. 1999. *The Material Life of Human Beings: Artifacts, Behavior, and Communication*. London: Routledge.

Schmidt, Martin, and Uta Halle. 1999. On the folklore of the Externsteine, or a centre for Germanomaniacs. In *Archaeology and Folklore*, eds. A. Gazin-Schwartz and C. Holtorf, 158–74. London: Routledge.

Schnapp, Alain. 1996. *The Discovery of the Past: The Origins of Archaeology*. London: British Museum Press.

Schneider, Arnd. 1993. The art diviners. *Anthropology Today* 9, no. 2:3–9.

Schneider, Lambert. 1985. Pfade zu uns selbst? Archäologie und Spurensicherung. *Kunst + Unterricht* 90 (February):8–14.

———. 1999. Das Pathos der Dinge. Vom archäologischen Blick in Wissenschaft und Kunst. In *Archäologie zwischen Imagination und Wissenschaft: Anne und Patrick Poirier*, ed. B. Jussen, 51–82. Göttingen: Wallstein.

Schörken, Rolf. 1995. *Begegnungen mit Geschichte: Vom außerwissenschaftlichen Umgang mit der Historie in Literatur und Medien*. Stuttgart: Klett-Cotta.

Schuldt, Ewald. 1972. *Die mecklenburgischen Megalithgräber. Untersuchungen zu ihrer Architektur und Funktion*. Berlin: Deutscher Verlag der Wissenschaften.

Schulze, Gerhard. 1993. *Die Erlebnis-Gesellschaft: Kultursoziologie der Gegenwart*. 3rd ed. Frankfurt: Campus.

Seidenspinner, Wolfgang. 1993. Archäologie, Volksüberlieferung, Denkmalideologie. Anmerkungen zum Denkmalverständnis der Öffentlichkeit in Vergangenheit und Gegenwart. *Fundberichte aus Baden-Württemberg* 18:1–15.

Service, Alexandra. 1998a. Vikings and Donald Duck. In *History and Heritage:*

Consuming the Past in Contemporary Culture, eds. J. Arnold, K. Davies, and S. Ditchfield, 17–26. Shaftesbury: Donhead.

———. 1998b. Popular Vikings: Constructions of Viking identity in twentieth-century Britain. Unpublished doctoral dissertation, University of York.

Shanks, Michael. 1990. Reading the signs: responses to archaeology after structuralism. In *Archaeology after Structuralism*, eds. I. Bapty and T. Yates, 294–310. London: Routledge.

———. 1992. *Experiencing the Past: On the character of archaeology*. London: Routledge.

———. 1995. Archaeological experiences and a critical romanticism. In *Nordic TAG. The Archaeologist and His/Her Reality. Report from the fourth Nordic TAG conference, Helsinki 1992*, eds. M. Tusa and T. Kirkinen, 17–36. University of Helsinki: Department of Archaeology.

———. 1996. *Classical Archaeology of Greece: Experiences of the discipline*. London: Routledge.

———. 1998. The life of an artefact in an interpretive archaeology. *Fennoscandia Archaeologica* 15:15–30.

———. 2001. Culture/archaeology: the dispersion of a discipline and its objects. In *Archaeological Theory Today*, ed. I. Hodder, 284–305. Cambridge: Polity.

Shanks, Michael, and Randall McGuire. 1996. The craft of archaeology. *American Antiquity* 61:75–88.

Shepherd, Nick. 2002. Heading south, looking north: why we need a post-colonial archaeology. *Archaeological Dialogues* 9:74–82.

Silberman, Neil. 1995. Promised lands and chosen people: the politics and poetics of archaeological narrative. In *Nationalism, Politics and the Practice of Archaeology*, eds. P. Kohl and C. Fawcett, 249–62. Cambridge: Cambridge University Press.

Silverman, Helaine. 2002. Groovin' to ancient Peru. *Journal of Social Archaeology* 2:298–322.

Spence, Donald. 1987. *The Freudian Metaphor: Toward Paradigm Change in Psychoanalysis*. New York: Norton & Co.

Stille, Alexander. 2002. *The Future of the Past*. London: Picador.

Storey, John. 2001. *Cultural Theory and Popular Culture: An Introduction*. 3rd ed. Harlow: Prentice Hall.

Talalay, Lauren. Forthcoming. The past as commodity: archaeological images in modern advertising. *Public Archaeology*.

Taylor, Mark, and Esa Saarinen. 1994. *Imagologies: Media Philosophy*. London: Routledge.

Thelen, David. 1989. Memory and American History. *The Journal of American History* 75:1117–29.

Thoden van Velzen, Diura. 1996. The world of Tuscan tomb robbers: living with the local community and the ancestors. *Cultural Property* 5:111–26.

———. 1999. The continuing reinvention of the Etruscan myth. In *Archaeology and Folklore*, eds. A. Gazin-Schwartz and C. Holtorf, 175–95. London: Routledge.

Thomas, Charles. 1976. The archaeologist in fiction. In *To Illustrate the Monuments: Essays on Archaeology Presented to Stuart Piggott*, eds. J. V. S. Megaw, 310–19. London: Thames and Hudson.

Thomas, Julian. 1996. *Time, Culture & Identity: An Interpretive Archaeology.* London: Routledge.

———. 2004. *Archaeology and Modernity.* London: Routledge.

Thomas, Roger. 1991. Drowning in data?—publication and rescue archaeology in the 1990s. *Antiquity* 65:822–28.

Thompson, Paul. 1988. *The Voice of the Past: Oral History.* 2nd ed. Oxford: Oxford University Press.

Tilley, Christopher. 1989a. Archaeology as sociopolitical action in the present. In *Critical Traditions in Contemporary Archaeology*, eds. V. Pinsky and A. Wylie, 104–16. Cambridge: Cambridge University Press.

———. 1989b. Excavation as theatre. *Antiquity* 63:275–80.

———. 1990. On modernity and archaeological discourse. In *Archaeology after Structuralism*, eds. I. Bapty and T. Yates, 128–52. London: Routledge.

———. 1993. Interpretation and a poetics of the past. In *Interpretative Archaeology*, ed. C. Tilley, 1–27. Oxford: Berg,

. 1996. *An Ethnography of the Neolithic: Early Prehistoric Societies in Southern Scandinavia.* Cambridge: Cambridge University Press.

Traxler, Hans. 1983. *Die Wahrheit über Hänsel und Gretel.* Reinbek: Rowohlt.

Trümpler, Charlotte, ed. 2001. *Agatha Christie and Archaeology.* London: British Museum Press.

Tunbridge, John, and Greg Ashworth. 1996. *Dissonant heritage: the management of the past as a resource in conflict.* Chicester: Wiley and Sons.

Ucko, Peter. 2001. Unprovenanced material culture and Freud's collection of antiquities. *Journal of Material Culture* 6:269–322.

Vandenberg, Philipp. 1977. *Auf den Spuren unserer Vergangenheit. Die größten Abenteuer der Archäologie.* München: Goldmann.

Vayne, Julian. 2003. Holding back the years. *The Cauldron* 107 (February):12–16.

Veit, Ulrich, Tobias Kienlin, Christoph Kümmel, and Sascha Schmidt, eds. 2003. *Spuren und Botschaften: Interpretationen materieller Kultur.* Münster: Waxmann.

Verne, Jules. 1994. *Journey to the Centre of the Earth* [1864]. Harmondsworth: Penguin.

Vernissage. 1999. Die klassische Kopie. Goethes zweites Gartenhaus. *Vernissage* 5:1999.

Voss, Jerome. 1987. Antiquity imagined: cultural values in archaeological folklore. *Folklore* 98:80–90.

Wallace, Jennifer. 2004. *Digging the Dirt: The Archaeological Imagination*. London: Duckworth.

Wallace, Mike. 1985. Mickey Mouse history: portraying the past at Disney World. *Radical History Review* 32:33–57.

Watrall, Ethan. 2002. Digital pharaoh: archaeology, public education and interactive entertainment. *Public Archaeology* 2:163–69.

Wetzel, Andreas. 1988. Reconstructing Carthage: archeology and the historical novel. *Mosaic* 21:13–23.

Whitley, James. 1997. Beazley as theorist. *Antiquity* 71:40–47.

Whittaker, John, and Michael Stafford. 1999. Replicas, fakes, and art: the twentieth century Stone Age and its effects on archaeology. *American Antiquity* 64:203–14.

Wienberg, Jes. 1999. The perishable past: on the advantage and disadvantage of archaeology for life. *Current Swedish Archaeology* 7:183–202.

Wijesuriya, Gamini. 2001. "Pious vandals": restoration or destruction in Sri Lanka? In *Destruction and Conservation of Cultural Property*, eds. R. Layton, P. Stone, and J. Thomas, 256–63. London: Routledge.

Wilk, Richard. 1985. The ancient Maya and the political present. *Journal of Anthropological Research* 41:307–26.

Williams, Raymond. 1976. *Keywords*. London: Fontana.

———. 1990. *Notes on the Underground: An Essay on Technology, Society and the Imagination*. Cambridge, Mass.: MIT Press.

Wolf, Ernest, and Sue Nebel. 1978. Psychoanalytic excavations: the structure of Freud's cosmography. *American Imago* 35:178–202.

Wood, Chris. 2002. The meaning of Seahenge. *3rd Stone* 43:49–54.

Woodall, Ned, and Philip Perricone. 1981. The archeologist as cowboy: the consequence of professional stereotype. *Journal of Field Archaeology* 8:506–9.

Woodward, Christopher. 2001. *In Ruins*. London: Random House.

Yarrow, Thomas. 2003. Artefactual persons: the relational capacities of persons and things in the practice of excavation. *Norwegian Archaeological Review* 36:65–73.

Zarmati, Louise. 1995. Popular archaeology and the archaeologist as hero. In *Gendered Archaeology: The Second Australian Women in Archaeology Conference*, eds. J. Balme and W. Beck, 43–47. Canberra: ANH Publications.

Zintzen, Christiane. 1998. *Von Pompeji nach Troja: Archäologie, Literatur und Öffentlichkeit im 19. Jahrhundert*. Wien: WUV Universitätsverlag.

INDEX

Acropolis, Athens, *10*, 157
adventures, 104–6. *See also* archaeology, as adventure; fieldwork, as adventure
advertisements, 45, *86*, *128*
age value, 113, 129, 146
Alaska, 48
Alltagskultur, 7
ancient astronauts, 11
antiquities, collection of, 74
Antwerp Zoo, Belgium, *10*, *152*
appeal, animal, 153. *See also* archaeo-appeal
archaeo-appeal, 14–15, 104, 150, 152, 155–57, 159, 160
archaeoastronomers, 133
archaeologists: armchair, 39; as detectives, 33, 60–63, 159; as heroes, 33, 56–57, 156; most famous in popular culture, *43–44*; as villains, 51
archaeology: as adventure, 42, 44, 50, 106, 139; allegiances of, 14; applied, 6; as birth, 35, 37; clichés of, 158; as erotic desire, 74; as experience, 135, 155–57, 160; and fashion, *41*–42; and masculinity, 40; as metaphor, 1–2, 25; as process and desire, 72–77; as propaganda, 51; as rescue, 37; secrets of, 13; and the sexes, 42; as treasure hunting, 53–54, 72; urban, 48

archäologischer Tatsachenroman (fact-based fiction), 56
architecture, 136
Arnesen, Britt, ix, 28, 39, 115–17
art, 12, 18, 33, 112–13, 121, 136–*37*. *See also Spurensicherung* art
art historians, 70
art history, 63
Articus, Charles Lightning, *43*
artifacts, 29, 116, 134, 148; as material clues, *76*
artists, 89–90. *See also* art
Ashworth, Greg, 127, 133, 148
Aster, Marla, *44*
Aston, Mick, 27. *See also Time Team*
Atlantis, 11
aura, 115, 118–19; of monuments, 106–7, 111; of objects, 115–16, 119, 127, 147
Australia, 33
authentic: copies, 119–27; experiences of the past, 128–29, 135–36. *See also* replicas; reproductions
authenticity, 15, 69, 107, 111–30, 140–42, 159
Avebury, Wiltshire, 90

Bagnall, Gaynor, 115, 140
Bahn, Paul, 74
Barrett, John, 70, 73
Basedow, 89

Battle of the Beanfield, 85
Beardsworth, Alan, 140, 153
Beazley, John, 63
Beltane, 105
Beltz, Robert, 89
Bender, Barbara, 63, 84
Ben Hur, 141
Benjamin, Walter, 115
Berger, John, 154
Bergman, Charles, ix, 133
Berlin Wall, 147
Bibby, Geoffrey, 56
biographies, of things, 79. *See also* life
    histories
Birt, Theodor, 21
Blieskastel, Saarland, *10*, 92, 99, 101,
    107. *See also* Gollenstein
bodies, *17*. *See also* Earth, as body
Boltanski, Christian, 65
Bond, James, 46
Borbein, Adolf, 73
Bordo, Omero, 126
Bradley, Richard, 83, 86
Bronze Age, 29, 81, 84–85, 87, 92,
    101, 106; barrows, 84, 87; cemetery,
    58
Bryman, Alan, 138, 140, 153
Burger, Phillip, 124
Burg Schlitz, Mecklenburg, 89
burial, *17*, 84; mounds, 87, 88, 101. *See
    also* Bronze Age, barrows;
    megaliths; Neolithic, long barrows
Burroughs, Edgar Rice, 23, 124
Butler, Samuel, 81

Caesars Palace, Las Vegas, 54, 143
Carnarvon, Jonathan, *44*
Carnarvon, Lord, 51
Carter, Howard, 28, 51, 53, 56

casino-hotels, 46, *142*–43. *See also* Las
    Vegas
Casson, Stanley, 62
cave paintings, 22
Ceram, C. W., 56
Cerne Giant, Dorset, 62
Champollion, Jean-François, 56
Chesil Beach, Dorset, *10*, 123
Chessington World of Adventures,
    152, 156. *See also* theme parks
Chippindale, Christopher, 84
Christianization, 88, 108
Christie, Agatha, 34, 54, 61
clichés, cultural, 141. *See also*
    archaeology, clichés of
clues, 63, 65, 68, 70, 75, 77, 83. *See
    also* traces as clues
comics, 45
commerce, 96–97. *See also*
    merchandising
computer games, 42, 44–45, 135
conservation: of ancient remains, 113,
    135, 144; animal, 151, 153; ethic,
    146; wildlife, 133
consumption, 138–39
copies, 112, 116, 134; original,
    125–26. *See also* authentic, copies;
    replicas; reproductions
Cortés, Hernando, 56
Crater, Robert, *44*
Cresswell, Tim, 97
criminology, 60–61, 70, 74. *See also*
    detectives
Croft, Lara, 42–*45*, *151*
cultural heritage, 134

Daniel, Glyn, 62
Dante, 22
Darvill, Timothy, 63, 130

Day, David, 42
decay, 146
deep time, *17*, 21
Dehio, Georg, 113
demolition, of monuments, 89. *See also* vandalism
destruction, of archaeological sites, 144–48
detectives, 34, 70, 157; as archaeologists, 60. *See also* archaeologists, as detectives
Devil, 88, 89
dig, mock archaeological, *55*, 152. *See also* excavation, simulated
digging, 30, 33–34, 39, 48; as archaeological theory, 58; as metaphor, 30. *See also* excavation
Ding, Indiana, *43*
Dion, Mark, 65–66, *68*, 69
dioramas, 135
discovery, *17*, 53–59, 69, 156, 159
Discovery Channel, 77, 141
Disney, Walt, 138. *See also* Disneyland; Donald Duck; Jöns, Indiana; Mickey Mouse; theme parks; Walt Disney World
Disneyization, 153, 157. *See also* history, Disneyfied
Disneyland, *10*; Adventureland, 139. *See also* theme parks; Walt Disney World
District Six, Cape Town, *10*, 32; museum, 33
Donald Duck, 105
Dörpfeld, Wilhelm, 57
dowsing, 11. *See also* Earth, mysteries
Doyle, Arthur Conan, 63
druids, 85, 109, 122, 133
Dummertevitz, Rügen, 86

Earhart Project, 77
Earth: as body, 34–37; mysteries, 109
Earthwatch, 37
Edgeworth, Matthew, 58
Edwards, Brian, 90
elsewhereness, 141
Emerson, Radcliffe, *44*
The Emperor's New Groove, 141
Empirische Kulturwissenschaft, vii
Erickson, Clark, 6
Erlebnis Zoo, Hannover, *10*, 152, 156
Etna, Sicily, *10*, 20
Etruscopolis, 127
Evans, Arthur, 56
Eversley, Robert, *43*
excavation: ethnography of, 58; as rape, 35; simulated, 156. *See also* dig, mock archaeological; digging; fieldwork
exotic locations, 44, 48, 151, 156
experiences. *See* archaeology, as experience
explorers, urban, 47

fables, 106. *See also* folk tales; legends
fakes, 107, 118, 121, 126, 133, 139. *See also* copies; replicas
Feder, Kenneth, 11
fiction: archaeological, fact-based, 56; literary, 1, 45. *See also* movies; novels
fieldwork, *59*; as adventure, 39–44, 59, 157, 159; dangers of, 15, 40, 46, 48–51, 53; hardships of, 46, 48, 55; as materializing practice, 58; as military campaign, 40. *See also* digging; excavation
Flag Fen, *10*, 54–*55*
Fletcher, Edward, 26

flint-knapping demonstrations, 106
folk: archaeology, 11; culture, 7; memory, 82; tales, 1, 26, 89; traditions, 26. *See also* fables; legends
folklore, 11–12, 46, 113, 153; of archaeological artifacts, 11; of archaeological monuments, 11, 89
forensic: archaeology, 62; science, 65
Foucault, Michel, 34
Fox, Sydney, 42–*43*
Freud, Sigmund, 31, 50, 60, 64–65, 74. *See also* psychoanalysis
Friedrich, Caspar David, 89, 103
Friends of the Earth International, 37
Fritz, J. M., 104
Furuviksparken, Gävle, *10*, 152, 154

Galen, Richard, *44*
Gardiner, Julie, 84
Gdansk, *10*, 125, 136
genealogy, 87–88
geology, 21
Georgia, *10*, 49
Gere, Cathy, 25
Geschichtskultur (culture of history), 5, 80, 91
Gette, Paul-Armand, 65
giants, 89
Ginzburg, Carlo, 63–65
Gladiator, 143
globalization, 9
Goethe, Wolfgang von, 122
Goethe's Garden House, Weimar, *10*, 122–23
Gollenstein, Blieskastel, Saarland, *10*, 92–94, 99, 100–103, 105, 107–9
Goof, Arizona, *43*
Goof, Indiana, *43*

Gorsedd of Bards, 136
Gottdiener, Mark, 141
graffiti, 100
Grinsell, Leslie, 26
guided tours, 95
Gulf War, 51

Hagenbeck, Carl, 153
Hamberge, Mecklenburg, 88
Hammurabi, 51
Harding, Phil, 42. *See also Time Team*
Harley-Davidson motorcycles, 124
Havelock, Melina, *43*
Hawkes, Jacquetta, 84
Hedenhös family, 156
Heid, Klaus, 118. *See also* Khuza culture
Heimat, 102
heritage: fabricated, 140; tourism, 97
hero. *See* archaeologists, as heroes
high culture, 7
Hill, Tobias, 32, 49
Hiller, Susan, 65
historical: research, 74; value, 113; veracity, 140
historic plays, 136
history: artificial, 4; Disneyfied, 139; false, 139; living, 136, 141. *See also Geschichtskultur*
Hollywood, 156
Holmes, Sherlock, 63–64, 157
Homer, 57
Hue, Vietnam, *10*, 146, 148
Hussein, Saddam, 51
Hutton, James, 20
Hutton, Ronald, 63
hyperreality, 140

Ice Man, 61
identities: collective, 32, 100–101,

134; national, 32; personal, 100;
social, 87, 102
identity: individual, 140; universal
human, 102
ideologies, 111, 134
Indiana Jones and the Temple of Doom,
36, 139
information boards, 95
International Council of Monuments
and Sites (ICOMOS), 113–14
Internet, 157
Iron Age, 29, 81, 84, 87–88, 106, 123;
burial mound, 101; hill fort, 123

Jackson, Daniel, *43*
Jacobs, Igshaan, 33
Jensen, Ola, 83
Johnson, Mark, 16, 146–47
Jones, Andy, 79
Jones, Indiana, 8, *36*, *43*–44, 139, *151*,
155–57
Jöns, Indiana, *43*
Jorvik, York, *10*, 155
Jungk, Robert, 124

Kalinowski, Konstanty, 125
Karlsminde. *See* Waabs-Karlsminde
Kastner, Lucien, *43*
Kemper, Steven, 149
Khuza culture, 8, 118
Kidder, Alfred, 40
Kilroy, Professor, *43*
Kinomoto, Fujitaka, *43*
Knossos, Crete, *10*, 64, *126*
Kopytoff, Igor, 79
Krieger, Martin, 133

Lahren, Larry, 42
Lake Titicaca, 6, *10*
Lakoff, George, 16

Lang, Nikolaus, 65
Lascaux, Dordogne, *10*, 22, *28*
Las Vegas, x, *10*, 13, 136, 138, 141–43,
156, 158, 160. *See also* Caesars
Palace; Luxor Hotel
Layard, Henry, 56
legends, 106, 153. *See also* fables; folk,
tales; myths; sagas
legislation, 113
Leidner, Eric, *43*
Lesser, Wendy, 25
Lewis, C. S., 22
ley hunters, 133
ley-lines, 11, 109. *See also* Earth,
mysteries
lieux d'archéologie, 15
lieux de mémoire (realms of memory), 4
life histories: of ancient sites, 146; of
individuals, 100; of prehistoric
objects, 83, 146; of Stonehenge, 84;
of things, 78, 80, 115
Lintilla, *43*
Lisch, Friedrich, 89
Littlejohn, William Harper, *43*
Lochhead, Alison, ix, *36*
London Underground, 32
looting, 148. *See also* tomb robbing
Lowenthal, David, 117, 123
Lucas, Gavin, ix, 58, 74
Luxor Hotel, Las Vegas, *142*–43

Macauley, David, *70*
Maiden Castle, Dorset, *10*, 123
Malamud, Margaret, 143
Mallowan, Max, 34, 54
Maltby, Richard, 8
Marek, Kurt W., 56
mass: culture, 7; media, 157. *See also*
television programs

materiality, 111–12, 119, 127, 129

meanings: contemporary, of monuments, 15, 91–111; past, 78–91, 159; secondary, 78; of things, 80

Mecklenburg-Vorpommern, *10*, 81, 84, 88–89

megaliths, vii, 4, 78, 83–95, 97–98, 100, 102, 105

memories: collective, 159; cultural, 80

memory, 2–4, 31. *See also* folk, memory

menhirs, 92–95, 99–103, 105, 107–8, 118, *120*–21

merchandising, 138. *See also* commerce; souvenirs

Merchant, Carolyn, 35

Mesopotamia, 61

metaphors, 16–17, 74–75, 132, 140, 144, 156, 159. *See also* archaeology, as metaphor; underground, as metaphor

Metken, Günther, 72

Mickey Mouse, 67

modernism, 144–45

Monte da Igreja, Portugal, viii, *10*, *23*

Monte Polizzo, Sicily, viii, *10*, 29, 47–48

Montgomery, Scott, 151

monumentality, 93–95

monuments: interpretations of, 111; as magical places, 107–9; metaphorical significance of, 98; as metaphors, 104; reception of, 97; reinterpretation of, 83. *See also* aura, of monuments; demolition, of monuments; folklore, of archaeological monuments; meanings, contemporary, of monuments; megaliths; menhirs

Morelli, Giovanni, 63–64

Morris, Desmond, 153–54

Moser, Stephanie, ix, 39, 42

movies, 1, 36, 42–45, 51, 139, 141, 143

The Mummy, 51

Museums Kopi Smykker, 125

Mycenae, *10*, 31

Mystère, Martin, *44*

mysteries, 33, 55. *See also* archaeologists, as detectives; novels, detective

myths, 23–24, 51, 142

Nagatani, Patrick, ix, 28

nationalism, 51

Native American Graves Protection and Repatriation Act, 33

Nebel, Sue, 31

Nebuchadnezzar, 51

Neidhardt, Markus, 125

Neolithic, 80, 83, 84, 90; artifacts, 79; burial, 86–87; long barrows, 92, 94, 95, 97, 100, 102, 106–7; mounds, 87; stone axes, 80–83

New Age followers, 106, 133. *See also* pagan rituals

Nobbin, Rügen, 88

Nora, Pierre, 4, 15

nostalgia, 87, 109–10, 156

novels, 9, 32, 42; about archaeologists, *43–44*, 46, 55; detective, *43–44*, 60, 61; (pre-)historic, 12. *See also* fiction, literary

Obelix, 105

O'Connell, Evelyn, *44*

Oldenburg, Claes, *18*

open-air museums, archaeological, 136, 157

oral history, 3, 30
originals, 112, 115–16, 123, 126
Ostia, Italy, *10*, 71, 147
otherness, 13–14, 141
Ouzman, Sven, 144

pagan rituals, 108
pagans, 35, 85, 122
Pallottino, Massimo, 26, 60, 62, 72
Parthenon, Nashville, Tennessee, 125
past: authentic, 118, 135; falsifying
    the, 124; as a nonrenewable
    resource, 15,129; perception of,
    118; personal, 3; in the present,
    158; as a renewable resource,
    130–49, 159; renewing the, 144,
    148, 159; secrets of the, 33, 48, 50
pastness, 127, 129–30, 159
Peabody, Amelia, *44*
Peacock, Alan, 132, 135
Petersson, Bodil, 106
Petrie, William, 56
Picard, Jean-Luc, *44*
pilgrims, 108
Pipps, Indiana, *43*
Pitt-Rivers, Augustus, 40
Poirier, Anne, ix, 65, 70–71, *73*
Poirier, Patrick, ix, 65, 70–71, *73*
Poirot, Hercule, 34, 61–62, 63
political parties, 133
Pompeii, *10*, 54, 64, 157
Poor, Nigel, ix, 65–*66*
Pörtner, Rudolf, 56
Powell, John, 40
preservation, 5, 99, 113, 130, 135
preservationists, 133
progress, 110–11; historical, *17*
Pryor, Francis, 27–28, 54
pseudoscience, 11

psychoanalysis, 31, 50, 60, 64, 70, 74.
    See also Freud, Sigmund
pyramids, 143, 157

rebred animal species, 136
reconstructions, 100, 125, 134, 136,
    155–56; virtual, 135
reenactments, 136
Relic Hunter, 42
reliving (pre-)history, 106
remembering, 72. *See also* memory
remote sensing techniques, 22
replicas, *76*, 107, 118–23, 125, 136,
    149. *See also* copies; reproductions
reprints of ancient texts, 136
reproductions, 115, 123–24, 143. *See
    also* copies; replicas
rescue archaeology, 130–31. *See also*
    archaeology, as rescue
restoration, 100, 113, 136, 145, 149
retro-chic, 136
reuse: of artifacts 81, 146; of
    monuments 87–88, 146
rhizomatic thinking, 19
Riegl, Alois, 113
Robinson, Tony, 27, 75. *See also Time
    Team*
Robson, Professor, *44*
Rock, Will, *44*
rock engravings, African, 145, 148
Rollins, James, 46
Roman: artifacts, 29; period, 54, 84,
    141
Romantic: painters, 89; poets, 89
Rome, 64
Rügen, *10*, 86, 88, 90
ruins, *52*, *73*, 136, 151
Rüsen, Jörn, 5
Russell, Miles, 11, 51

Saalburg, Hessen, *10*, 54
Saarinen, Esa, 19
sagas, 26. *See also* folk, tales; legends
Sam Hill, Maryhill, Washington, *10*, 122
San Diego Wild Animal Park, *10*, *151*
Sargon the Great, 51
Schadla-Hall, Tim, ix, 123
Schiffer, Michael, 79
Schliemann, Heinrich, 24, 31, 50, 56–57, 157
Schuldt, Ewald, 90
Schulze, Gerhard, 121, 157
science fiction, 11. *See also* novels
Seahenge, Holme-next-the-Sea, 35
Sea World, 152, 154
Segesta, Sicily, *10*, 147
Seidenspinner, Wolfgang, 10
Service, Alexandra, 141
Shanks, Michael, viii, 16, 35, 62, 115, 121, 135
Simonds, Charles, 65
social: power, 98; prestige, 87
souvenirs, 136. *See also* copies, original; merchandising
Spence, Donald, 74
sphinx, 143
Sprockhoff, Ernst, 90
Spurensicherung art, 65–73, 77. *See also* art
stone: circles, modern, 136; robbers, 90
Stonehenge, x, *10*, 13, 84–85, 98, 102, 108, 136, 160
Stonehenge III, 122
stratigraphy, 21
stupas, 145, 148
Summerfield, Bernice, *44*
summer solstice, 85

Taragon, Hercules, *44*
Taylor, Mark, 19

television programs, 9, 27, 42–45, 75, 141, 158
temples, artificial, 136, *152*
themed environments, 155–56
theme parks, 1, 46, 155; Disney, 118, 136, 138–41, 151–52, 155. *See also* Chessington World of Adventures
theming, 138, 140–41, 151, 155
Thomas, Julian, ix, 79
Thompson, Edwards, 56
Thompson, Paul, 30, 34
Tilley, Christopher, 79
Time Team, 42, 75
Tomb Blaster, 156
Tomb Raider, 42. *See also* Croft, Lara
tomb robbing, 12, 148
tourism, 1, 25, 102, 118, 157; and authenticity, 118
toys, 46, *52*
traces as clues, 15, 60, 69, 75, 91
treasure hunters, 25, 27, 44, 50, 90. *See also* archaeology, as treasure hunting; tomb robbing
treasures, 15, 25–28, 31, 33–34, 39, 46, 50, 55, 157, 159; as metaphor, 25–26, 39
treasure trove, 26
tree-thinking, 16, 19
Troy, *10*, 24
Tübingen-Weilheim, Baden-Württemberg, *10*, 92, *94*–95, 97, 99–101, 103, 107, 109, 118, *120*
Tunbridge, John, 127, 133, 148
Tutankhamun's tomb, 27–28, 51, 53, 143
Twain, Mark, 22

underground, 15–38, 39, 50, 156–57, 159; as metaphor, 16, 22, 38, 49

Unesco, 114, 146
Unesco World Heritage Centre, 113, 130
Ur, *10*, 61
Utopias, 156

Valley of the Kings, Egypt, *10*, 53. *See also* Tutankhamun's tomb
vandalism, 146. *See also* destruction, of archaeological sites
Vandenberg, Philipp, 56
Vasa Museum, Stockholm, 155
Vasa ship, 119
Vash, *44*
Vayne, Julian, 146
Venice Charter, 113
Vernes, Jules, 22
Vikings, 81, 105, 106, 142
Virgil, 22
visitors from outer space, 11
Volkskunde, vii
Vorgeschichtskultur (culture of prehistory), 92
Voss, Jerome, 11

Waabs-Karlsminde, 92, 94, 96–97, 99, 102–3, 106–7

Wallace, Jennifer, 35
Wallace, Mike, 138
Walt Disney World, *10*; Animal Kingdom, 151–52. *See also* Disneyland; theme parks
Warburg, Aby, 71
Warsaw, 125, 136
Weilheim. *See* Tübingen-Weilheim
Wetzel, Andreas, 144
Wheeler, Mortimer, 40, 123
Wildwood Trust, Kent, 153, 156
Willey, Gordon, 62
Williams, Raymond, 7
Williams, Rosalind, 23–24, 33
Winckelmann, Johann Joachim, 113
Winslet, Kate, 19
Wolf, Ernest, 31
Wood, Miss, *44*
Wookey Hole Caves, Somerset, 25
Woolley, Leonard, 56, 61

Yarrow, Thomas, ix, 58, 117
York. *See* Jorvik, York

zoos, 150, 151, 154–55

ABOUT THE AUTHOR

Cornelius Holtorf (born 1968) works as an assistant professor in archaeology at the University of Lund in Sweden. He gained his doctoral degree from the University of Wales with a study of the life history of megalithic monuments in northeast Germany. After stints as an academic teacher and researcher at the Universities of Wales (Lampeter), Göteborg, and Cambridge, and a two-year Marie Curie Fellowship at the Swedish National Heritage Board in Stockholm, he recently moved to his current post at Lund. His research interests include the portrayal of archaeology in contemporary popular culture, excavations investigating the life history of a megalith at Monte da Igreja in southern Portugal, and the archaeology of zoos. He is the author of many academic papers and the "living" electronic monograph *Monumental Past* (2000–2004), and coeditor of *Archaeology and Folklore* (1999) and *Philosophy and Archaeological Practice* (2000).